Herblock's State of the Union

BY HERBERT BLOCK

Herblock's State of the Union

Herbert Block

Grossman Publishers
A Division of The Viking Press
New York   1974

To Doree
and Jean
and Jane

Contents

Author's Note:

In preparation for this paperback edition I reread *State of the Union* to see if there was anything in it I'd change beyond minor corrections. I found that in the hardcover printing, I had already made one change too many. At the end of the chapter "The Law-and-Order Gang" I had originally made a reference to "Corruption in the Very Highest Places." But in going over final proofs for that first edition, I decided that this might *seem* to be putting it too strongly; so I changed it to "Corruption in Very High Places."

I should have left it the way it was.

H. B.
April, 1974

26059

"... IT VANISHED QUITE SLOWLY, BEGINNING WITH THE END OF
THE TAIL, AND ENDING WITH THE GRIN, WHICH REMAINED SOME
TIME AFTER THE REST OF IT HAD GONE."
—ALICE AND THE CHESHIRE CAT

12/23/71

Foreword

DURING THE DARKEST DAYS *of World War II, Winston Churchill delivered a one-paragraph message to the people, which began: "The news from France is very bad. . . ."*

He could have done it differently. He could have said: "My fellow citizens: As your Prime Minister—and Prime Minister of <u>all</u> the people—I want to talk to you tonight, in my most sincere manner, about a problem which faces me as the man who holds the highest office in our land. I refer to the stories and speculations and rumors printed in the newspapers and broadcast over the air waves which would have you believe that conditions are not good, that we are in deep trouble, that all sorts of terrible things are happening. Now I respect the right of newsmen and commentators to have their say—false and vicious and slanderous as the things they say so often are. And though it is not the politically safe or easy thing to do, let me say candidly and clearly that I would not pretend for a moment that everything is absolutely perfect in this great country or this great world of ours. But I think you are probably as tired as I am of hearing our country and our allies run down by prejudiced people who do not represent the majority of our splendid citizens, and who never tell you about all the <u>good</u> things that are happening. As you know, it is my policy to act boldly and decisively in each and all of my many crises. Accordingly, I am now making to you an unprecedented announcement. This morning I appointed, for the first time in our nation's history, a Good News Commission. This Commission, which will have the full power of the nation's law-enforcement agencies behind it, will report directly to me. I will then . . ."

But enough.

The news from Washington is bad. ■

"BY THE POWERS VESTED IN ME, I HEREBY DECLARE EACH OF YOU
A SUCCESS."

10/30/70

PRolitics

WHENEVER people are frustrated by government, or weary of public speeches, they're likely to say, "It's all politics!" or "It's the same old politics!" By this they don't mean "the art of the possible" so much as the artful telling of the improbable. Actually we don't have the "same old politics" any more, especially since so many political TV spots have been served up, along with other harmful additives.

More and more, public relations techniques and PR men have moved into the field, and we now have PR politics, or PRolitics. Political commentator Albert Tannenbaum has even suggested that in 1969 we got our first PResident.

Anyhow, the Chief Executive now has not only a Press Secretary with staff, but a Director of Communications, a Deputy Director of Communications, and about fifty public relations men, right in the White House—not counting the hundreds in all the other departments of the executive branch.

So many advertising men, public relations people and former television executives have been brought in that any day now they may start referring to their headquarters as the Whiter-Than-White House—even though it doesn't always seem to come clean clean clean with us.

Actually, the White House *does* look whiter than ever, as do the other government buildings, which have been scrubbed down and absolutely gleam at night under lighting that is really whiter-and-brighter-than-ever. We may not be able to see what goes on inside those buildings any more, but the exterior illuminations are enough to knock your eyes out. That's what experienced ad men and TV crews can do.

For years, old words have been given new meanings, and euphemisms have been substituted for old words. "Conservative" used to be a perfectly respectable classification for those who held to traditions and much of the best of the past, including the Bill of Rights. It has been used lately as a category to include racists, politicians who want to throw around nuclear bombs, and those who have felt that President Eisenhower and President Nixon were procommunist. "Fighter against communism" is a term some of the same people have given themselves—a description, like "conservative," too often picked up by newspapers who generously apply such words to radicals and raving nuts.

The Indochina war has given us many euphemisms, including *incursion*. And here at home we may soon hear of "incursions of privacy."

We've had more than an ounce of *prevention* in phrases that carry a touch of Orwell. "Preventive strikes," "protective reaction" (not to mention "reinforced protective reaction") and "preventive detention" are all indirect descendants of such phrases as "protective custody"—a term first employed in

"ONLY WHEN I LAUGH"
11/6/70

"THERE'S AN ART TO
ANALYZING STATISTICS."
10/3/71

". . . IT WAS ANNOUNCED TODAY
THAT THE PRESIDENT HAD A
SECRET MEETING WITH
DR. KISSINGER TO DISCUSS FUTURE
SECRET MEETINGS ABOUT SECRET
MEETINGS WITH . . ."
5/19/72

"IT WAS A PROTECTIVE REACTION
AS PART OF A UNILATERAL
UNDERSTANDING TO MAINTAIN
A LOWER PROFILE AT A
HIGHER LEVEL."
11/26/70

some countries where dissidents were arrested, presumably to protect them from their own follies.

Prolitics has not only worked variations on words and phrases, but has given us some innovations in political practice. One of these is the *Preventive Event*. This involves a constant heralding of coming attractions, such as forthcoming Presidential trips or broadcasts. Criticism—or at least complete discussion—is constantly delayed or turned into a guessing game because Something Is Coming. If it's a speech, the announcement will go forth that the President will deliver a speech on this or that. It is going to be An Important One. We then hear that he is working on it. He's discussing it with his advisers. He's considering alternatives. He's going to define policy. Wait—Here it comes! *Here it is! WOW!* But don't go away—upcoming is an international meeting to discuss further steps, and likely to include new revelations. . . . His advisers are already meeting with advisers of other leaders. . . . New plans are being worked out. . . . Everyone will be well advised to hold his breath until . . .

In the 1968 campaign there was a kind of double-ploy *Preventive Peace-Plan Policy.* The candidate (a) would not say anything on the war because he did not wish to jeopardize President Johnson's negotiations; and (b) he had peace plans of his own which it would be premature to disclose publicly. These prevented the need to discuss present or future Vietnam policy. From the beginning of his presidency well into the fourth year, he continually gave the impression that we were on the very brink of a peace which might be endangered by any criticism or questioning.

Prolitics is not completely innovative, and usually builds its PR techniques onto political practices that have worked in the past. The country was fascinated by the energy and travels of Theodore Roosevelt; it was electrified when Franklin Roosevelt accepted his Presidential nomination without waiting weeks to be notified by a committee, but by going direct to the convention *by airplane.* With planes, Secretary of State John Foster Dulles probably logged more travel time than any previous high official, though the benefits of those travels were not always apparent.

From such beginnings was developed prolitics' *first law of motion:* Don't just sit there and *work*—do something. Thus, trips to San Clemente or Key Biscayne are news; meetings with leaders of other governments are spectaculars; and distinguished visitors to the White House can't face the cameras without the President waving his arms, pointing backward or forward, and grabbing the arms of these guests as if they could not find their way to the stairs without his help. This is all in accordance with the prolitical rule that Any Action Is Good, and travel is broadening to the voting base.

After the week-long live TV China travelogue, it took a prolitical production to keep the Russian summit trip from seeming anti-climactic. The White House brought to our screens *The Return From Moscow!* A joint meeting of Congress was called for 9:30 P.M. (Eastern Prime Time) to hear the President immediately on his return from Europe! The Presidential plane

"EVERYTHING'S FINE. LAST WEEK MY BOY
WAS WOUNDED IN THE VIETNAM PEACE;
YESTERDAY I WAS MUGGED ON THE STREETS
THAT ARE FREE OF FEAR; AND TODAY MY
HUSBAND WAS LAID OFF IN THE NEW PROSPERITY."

12/26/71

"GOOD NEWS! THE STATISTICS INDICATE DECREASES
IN THE RATES OF—UH—INCREASE . . ."

8/14/70

touched down at Andrews Air Force Base, where a helicopter waited. While Congress and TV viewers also waited, the Presidential helicopter flew to Capitol Hill, hovered over it, and set down in front of the Capitol itself!

The President and his wife emerged and chatted with their waiting family. Then all mounted the long flight of Capitol steps. Now as most visitors to Washington know, the Capitol is usually entered on the ground floor—where there are, of course, elevators. But the climbing of all those steps made more TV footage. One broadcaster confided to the viewers that the White House script had originally called for the President to mount the long flight of stairs alone. What a picture! But it might have left viewers wondering how his family got up there into the House chamber so much faster without that climb.

After the entrance of the family, finally came—yes—the President himself. And at last The Message! Did it contain anything new or startling? No. He could have spoken to Congress the next day or the next week. He could have sent over the message—or even mailed it.

But prolitics had provided the moment-by-moment Return From Moscow, with the members of the United States Congress serving as extras. Whatever the accomplishments of the summit itself, the return deserved an Oscar for the Most Dispensable Dramatic Production Of The Year.

Prolitics also provides the *Happening* or *Non-Event*. Example: photos in the newspapers of the Vice President standing at a podium, addressing the President and full cabinet (seated), and telling them what a great job they're doing; also similar photos and stories in which other officials tell each other how well they're all doing. I'm not making up any of this, honest.

This brings us to prolitical innovations that derive from Barnum, Bailey, Durstine & Osborne. It is a step up from modest exaggeration to *The Word-Shaking Event* and the *Triumph Of Title*. The astronauts' first landing on the moon was truly historic and sensational—but the President called it "the greatest achievement since Creation." One giant leap for mankind, one quantum jump for rhetoric.

When White House recommendations that included one more proposed reshuffling of government departments were billed as "The New American Revolution," this was a Triumph Of Title, though both "revolution" and title soon faded.

In one television appearance the President referred to the somewhat vague "Guam policy" as "what has been described as the Nixon Doctrine."

Shortly after his arrival in China he spoke of the "week that could change the world." And on the seventh day—he proclaimed it the "week that changed the world."

In a U.S. television interview he said that his first announcement of his forthcoming trip to China had been "what many think was the greatest surprise in history." This was not long after he had described an international currency agreement (on his own and without attribution to the anonymous

"CHIEF, I THINK WE'VE FOUND WHAT
WE'VE BEEN LOOKING FOR."

5/20/70

"NO PICTURES OF A CAPTURED ENEMY
HEADQUARTERS? WELL, HOW ABOUT BOILING THAT
CAPTURED RICE TO MAKE IT FLUFF UP MORE?"

6/5/70

"many") as "the most significant monetary agreement in the history of the world." Only an editorial cad would say, as one did, that it was the most significant monetary agreement since the last one.

The new agreement followed by some months a wage-price freeze and import tax which the same President merely put forth as the most important economic program in four decades—which would have been since 1931 and the days of Herbert Hoover.

Word-Shaking Events and Triumphs Of Title led inevitably to another distinctively prolitical policy: *Success By Proclamation*. This may have had its origin in a non-partisan and non-prolitical idea proposed by Senator George Aiken during the Johnson Administration. He suggested that the best way to get out of Vietnam was to say that we had won and achieved our objectives— and then leave.

In the lexicon of prolitics, there is no such word as *fail*.

Thus the 1969-71 Economic Game Plan was constantly declared a *success*, even as it was going under for the last time. *Peace* was hailed while Americans were still being shot in Indochina. And with unemployment running high, prosperity was not just around the corner—we were in a *New Prosperity*. Economics became a study of cause and special effects.

The 1970 off-year elections, in which the President's intervention proved of no avail, were officially declared a success—even if they were not the kind the President would want to see repeated in his own 1972 election.

PR men know that visual aids are always useful, and these have played a part in many simulated successes. If a high official displays actual maps of Cambodia or has economic charts he can point to, these are almost as useful as being able to show a faster pain-reliever dissolve in a glass stomach. An upward curve on a chart looks as if we're really going somewhere, even if the curve only represents a rise in the number of optimistic official statements. Increases in violent crime showed a *slowing in the rate of increase*. And when even that couldn't be said, then we were getting a higher class of violent crime —or something.

Some of the best examples of Success By Proclamation came in Indochina.

One of the reasons for our 1970 invasion of Cambodia was to find COSVN, the enemy communications headquarters, or nerve center, or Underground Pentagon. When we found only caches of rice and arms, we had achieved our objective.

Another great example of Success By Proclamation was the report of the raid on Sontay to bring back American prisoners of war.

Secretary of Defense Melvin Laird testified before a Senate committee, and before TV cameras, holding a photo of a small-scale model of the Sontay prison camp itself—presumably accurate in detail. He told how perfectly the raid had been planned, how well the raiding party was trained, how our helicopters had flown through holes in the enemy radar screens, and how the valorous men taking part in the raid had burst into the POW camp and gone about their assigned tasks with perfect precision! Our military intelligence, he proudly proclaimed, was excellent.

All this seemed confusing to some Senators who agreed on the valor and training of the men, but wondered if there might not have been something wrong with our military information—since the prisoners of war had been moved from the camp before our raid on it.

To this Secretary Laird replied, with a brilliant display of indignation, that we do not yet have cameras that can see through the rooftops of buildings.

To make the success complete, President Nixon had members of the raiding party brought to the White House, where they were presented with medals to honor their exploits behind enemy lines.

If such techniques had existed at the time of the battle of Balaklava, tributes to the "noble six hundred" might have completely obscured the fact that "someone had blundered" in ordering the Charge of the Light Brigade.

The Bay of Pigs plan was already well in the works before Senator John F. Kennedy became President, but he took full blame for the fiasco. I wonder what would have happened had he lost that election and had his opponent—and prolitical staff—been in office at the time. We might have had a press story something like this:

> WASHINGTON, D.C. April 21, 1961
> Defense Secretary Melvin Laird spoke today about the daring and brilliant attempt to retake Cuba through a landing of forces at the Bay of Pigs.

"IT'S LIKE NIXON SAID—THERE'S HARDLY ANYONE AROUND WHO HASN'T HELPED CHANGE A PUBLIC GOLF COURSE INTO A PRIVATE SEGREGATED CLUB."

2/1/70

"VIETNAMIZATION HAS BEEN SO SUCCESSFUL WE'VE DECIDED TO EXTEND IT."

5/3/70

"The men who engaged in this hazardous undertaking," he said, "were all volunteers. They were thoroughly trained, sometimes 16 to 18 hours a day. This mission was planned perfectly.

"President Nixon has personally thanked the men who displayed remarkable valor in this action. And if it had been possible for them to complete their objective, Cuba would now be well on its way to freedom."

Press Secretary Ron Ziegler said, "The President feels Castro is now on notice that the United States is no pitiful helpless giant. The President has expressed his pride and satisfaction over the splendid results of this bold move against communism, and has proclaimed next Monday as Salute The Volunteers Day. Had the mission accomplished its purpose, it would have been an even greater success."

When a prolitician is hard pressed, he may resort to the *Diverting Irrelevancy*. This proved useful when Americans felt bitter about the 1971 unopposed "election" of President Thieu. President Nixon noted sadly that if we refused to send representatives to the inaugurations of winners of uncontested elections around the world, we would have only one-third as many delegations to send. How true!—and how completely beside the point that General Thieu's regime had long been propped up by our government, which had supposedly brought democracy to Vietnam.

A similar example of the Diverting Irrelevancy followed disclosures about Judge G. Harrold Carswell's part in turning a public golf course into a private one. When President Nixon was asked about the Carswell record, he observed that if all those in government service who had belonged to a restricted golf club were to leave Washington, it would have the highest unemployment rate in the country. Such a ploy not only turns a phrase but turns the question too. Judge Carswell's problem was not merely that he had *belonged* to a private club, but had apparently tried to circumvent desegregation rulings by helping to form one.

A later court nomination fight brought into play an old but important prolitical device—*Preventive Disclosure*. This is based on the fact that it is not wrongdoing that is damaging, but *disclosure*.

The confirmation prospects for both Judge Carswell and Judge Haynsworth had suffered from continuous revelations about their records. When William Rehnquist's name was before the Senate, a reporter was about to break the story of an incident in which a judge had delivered a blistering reprimand to Rehnquist, accusing him of "highly reprehensible" legal conduct. This time the Administration itself quickly released the story—and a statement by the former judge (who had only shortly before received an Administration appointment) saying that what Rehnquist had done wasn't really so bad after all. Had there been no Preventive Disclosure, the newspaper revelation would have been damaging.

When it is too late for Preventive Disclosure, an artful prolitician can try simulating it. This requires real finesse. Mr. Nixon managed it when he was a United States Senator running for Vice President and *The New York Post* disclosed that he was the continuous beneficiary of a fund contributed to him by some California businessmen. The Senator was in hot water. But in his famous Checkers speech he said that there was nothing secret about the fund. And, to be sure, there wasn't anything secret about it—*after it had been disclosed in the newspapers.* But the impression was that it had always been public knowledge. This was a skillful example of *ex post facto* Preventive Disclosure.

Since timing is of the essence in these matters, the next best thing to do-it-yourself disclosure is to accuse the disclosers of *badly-timed* disclosures. In October 1968, *The New York Times* revealed that an investigation of Governor Spiro Agnew's record as local, county, and state official in Maryland showed conflicts of interest, which it cited specifically. The reply was that the disclosures (a) were old charges, already aired; and (b) came so late in the campaign that they constituted a "smear." Thus *The New York Times* was accused of being too late in every respect with its disclosures—as if it were a gin-rummy player sneaking something from the bottom of the discard. Lost in the shuffle were the newspaper's *facts,* which showed Mr. Agnew's political ethics to be very questionable indeed. Actually, they'd never had a real airing, though they could certainly have used some fresh air.

Much of prolitics is simply the same old politics practiced with a special daring or an extra flair for PR effect.

When former President Johnson said in 1971 that he felt he just hadn't communicated properly, he may not have realized that the difference was in having "Directors of Communications" and the techniques of *prolitics.* LBJ

©1972 HERBLOCK

"YOU DON'T UNDERSTAND, SON. WHEN
DEMOCRATS GO THERE, IT'S A SELLOUT—
WHEN WE GO, IT'S A JOURNEY FOR PEACE."
5/23/72

could whip out polls which favored his policies, and could pooh-pooh polls when they seemed unfavorable. President Nixon could be just as inconsistent, but with an added touch. When asked about mail which was running against something he wanted, he could recall that "I always used to tell young senators when they first came to Washington that in making a decision, they should do it not by weighing the mail but by weighing the evidence." But, lo! When it seemed important to show a favorable response, there were photographs of sacks of mail on White House tables, with percentages on how pro-President they ran.

Other Presidents have taken "nonpolitical" trips around the country which did them no harm politically, and have embarked on them with a broad wink. But President Nixon developed to its highest degree the art of *Rising Above Politics While Taking It With You.* After the 1970 campaign, he said in a TV interview that he was not wearing his political hat in off-years like 1971. In a 1972 TV appearance, he was not going to engage in politics till after the conventions. And in delivering a 1972 message to Congress, he pleaded with the legislators to put politics aside.

But somehow or other—in these and his other appearances—he managed to convey the impression that everything was in terrible shape when he took over; that he had achieved peace with prosperity; and that he'd continue doing wonderful, unprecedented things for us, at home and abroad—if only those other fellows would stop playing politics with the national interest.

A prolitical ploy which has gained in popularity in the past few decades is the *Offensive Defense.* An example of this might be the assertion that one's opponent is squishy-soft on communism, but has not yet been proven to be a communist himself. A variation would be the charge by the Offensive Defender that an opponent has a vested interest in his country's defeat, followed by a statement that the opponent's patriotism is not under question.

In February 1972, there occurred an example of *Group Offensive* coupled with *Top-Level Offensive Defense.* It was directed primarily against Senator Edmund Muskie, considered then to be President Nixon's most likely opponent in the fall election, and it included other candidates who also expressed disagreement with Presidential policy on the war.

White House "chief of staff" H. R. Haldeman (former advertising executive) said, in a pre-taped segment of NBC's *Today* show, that critics of President Nixon's latest peace-proposal speech insisted on "putting a communist government in Vietnam" and were "consciously aiding and abetting the enemy"—a slight paraphrase of the Constitutional definition of treason.

Many Administration officials took part in the offensive, even including Secretary of State William Rogers, who professed to be "dismayed" by criticism and asserted it was harmful to peace negotiations. Senate stalwarts categorized criticism of the President as "gutter politics"; and Communications Director Herbert Klein accused Muskie of "bolting beyond the bounds of

"LET ME MAKE TWO THINGS CLEAR. FIRST: THE COUNTRY IS IN
FINE SHAPE. AND SECOND: CONGRESS IS TO BLAME FOR THE MESS
WE'RE IN."

8/2/70

criticism and dissent" and "toying with the lives of both Americans and Asians."

After this series of attacks had reached its climax, President Nixon delivered a speech in which he said, "I have no complaint over the fact that during the period when I have been ending the war I did not begin I have been subjected to vigorous criticism. I do not question the patriotism or the sincerity of those who disagree with my policies to bring peace. . . . " He then asserted that a candidate for President has a higher responsibility than the ordinary critic and should say nothing that might give the enemy an incentive to prolong the war until after the election.

Few prolitical generals would attempt so intricate a maneuver of Rising Above Politics to command the attack below, and of timing his personal Offensive Defense to avoid Peaking Too Soon—or at too high a level.

Despite all the techniques of prolitics, the credibility gap that existed during the Johnson Administration seemed, if anything, to widen under the Nixon Administration. And the chasm was not bridged by expanded terminologies, well-turned-and-twisted phrases, and circumlocutions.

By now I'm used to the fact that the President receives not advice or information but *input*. A word that signals a White House emergency situation is *misspoke*.

When the President has given out facts, figures or dates that are wrong, aides say that he "misspoke himself." This can cover a slip of the tongue or a statement that our marines built over 25,000 churches, pagodas, and temples for the people of Vietnam—which later turned out to be 117 churches and 251 schools.

A combination of what might be called *The Footless Statistic* and *Rising Above Politics While Taking It With You* occurred in June 1970, when the President berated Congress for taking no action on thirteen crime bills which he said he had sent within the past eighteen months. "I understand partisan politics," said Mr. Nixon. "I understand it is an election year. I can understand Congress dragging its feet about some things. After all, that is the way the political game is played. But respect for law, dealing with crime—these are issues that are above partisan politics."

Confused reporters found that the President did indeed "understand partisan politics" when they discovered a great variety of bills that might relate to crime—some of which were drafted by Congressmen themselves, some remaining from the Johnson Administration, but none from President Nixon as long ago as eighteen months. White House aides eventually replied to questions by saying the President referred to *any* thirteen bills that had not yet passed Congress.

President Nixon has said on television that he has no use for public relations and is not concerned about his "image." Certainly his image was not improved with members of the press who dug up the actual stories concerning statements like those on the crime bills. There was increasing talk of Government by Gimmick—or Telling It Like It Ain't.

But the facts about those crime bills took quite a while to run down. The true story wasn't pieced together overnight. What *did* happen overnight was that the President prepared another blast at Congress for another supposed failure. On the day after the "crime bill" accusation, President Nixon, with Secretary George Romney standing at his side, excoriated Congress for failing to act on a specific housing measure that he had proposed months before.

Said the President of the United States to the reporters assembled at the White House on the 12th of June, 1970:

> Ladies and gentlemen, on February 2, I sent to the Congress a message asking for the enactment of the Emergency Home Finance Act of 1970. You will note that I described this as the "Emergency" Home Finance Act of 1970. Four months have passed and the Congress has yet failed to act . . .

Shirley Elder, a Capitol Hill correspondent for *The Washington Star*, was bothered that she had not yet been able to run down the crime bills mentioned

The Weather

Today—Partly cloudy with the high near 80. Sunday—Fair, high near 80. Chance of rain, 20 per cent today, near zero tonight. Temperature range: Today, 65-79. Yesterday, 67-92. Details are on Page B11.

The Washi

6-13-70

Times B

93d Year · · · · No. 190   © 1970, The Washington Post Co.   SATURDAY, J

Housing 'Crisis' Is Cited

President, Hill Trade Blasts On Legislation

By Carroll Kilpatrick
Washington Post Staff Writer

For the second time in two days, President Nixon criticized Congress yesterday for failing to give him legislation he requested, and congressional leaders replied sharply.

The President said that a "crisis" had developed in the nation's housing program because Congress has delayed action on a measure he proposed in February.

On Thursday, the President assailed Congress for failure to complete action on any of the 13 anticrime bills he recommended.

Yesterday, after conferring with Secretary of Housing and Urban Development George Romney, Mr. Nixon told newsmen that "it is time to act, even at this late date" on the emergency housing act.

The debate between the Republican President and the congressional Democrats appeared to be setting the stage for the fall elections.

The sharpest rejoinders came to the President's housing statement, although Senate Democratic Leader Mike Mansfield (Mont.) also replied that the Senate had a good record on passing anticrime legislation.

Mansfield said that the Senate had passed 11 of the 13 anticrime bills. "He's blaming all of us," Mansfield said. "He ought to be more discriminating."

Senate Republican Leader Hugh Scott (Pa.) said that it was "the other body" that had been "delinquent" in passing anticrime bills.

Both House Democratic Leader Carl Albert, Chairman Wri-
Te-
r

Frank Johnston—The Washington Post

President Nixon stresses need for new housing as HUD Secretary Romney listens.

the day before. She now kicked herself for not having remembered that Emergency Housing Act sent to Congress on February 2. True, a Congressional reporter can't remember everything, but something so specific, something that the President obviously considered so important—

She looked through her notes, and then through the newspaper files and the issues of Presidential documents. Finally she called the White House.

To quote from her story of June 14, 1970:

> There was no White House message to Congress on Feb. 2 urging enactment of an emergency housing bill. There was a budget message. It touched briefly on housing, pointing to a need for 600,000 new units. It said nothing about specific legislation . . .

Miss Elder gave a chronology of events: When a House committee began hearings on February 2, no Administration position was offered. When Secretary Romney was invited to present the White House view, he was unable to attend a session till the end of February—and then could offer no definite plan. He said that "legislation is being prepared" but didn't say when it would be ready. *The Senate* went ahead and polished up the Emergency Home Finance Act of 1970, in April—and passed it unanimously.

Following this, the Administration for the first time let it be known that it favored this bill. "As of yesterday," said Miss Elder's middle-of-June article, "a committee spokesman said there had been no sign of a presidential housing message or a White House bill"—and Congressmen expressed irritation at Administration delays.

"SOMEBODY'S DRAGGING HIS FEET!"
6/16/70

**"WELL, IT'S PRETTY
REVOLUTIONARY FOR US."**
2/2/71

**"WE'RE HAVING A REALLY GREAT
SEASON, EXCEPT FOR THE SCORES."**
7/30/71

ARMS RACE
5/26/72

As for the President's denunciation of Congress for not passing his non-existent proposal, a White House aide conceded that "if the President said that [the original statements], he misspoke himself. . . . That sometimes happens."

That sometimes happens in prolitics, where *misspeak* seems to be closely related to *newspeak*.

Perhaps one time when we should have given the greatest weight to words was early in the Administration, when Attorney General John Mitchell told an unhappy civil rights group, "You will be better advised to watch what we do than what we say."

What we do and say is noted abroad, as well as at home, and the credibility gap has not stopped at the water's edge. Confidence in our words to the world was not increased by the efforts of U.S. Information Agency head Frank Shakespeare—former Procter and Gamble executive and former TV executive—to politicize the USIA and to lard its statements with propaganda.

As the nation prepared to celebrate its 200th anniversary, we seemed to have come a long way from James Madison to Madison Avenue. The Presidential plane, which used to be known simply as Air Force 1, was christened the Spirit of '76—but it didn't say *which* '76. And as we got closer to 1984, we seemed to be missing the spirit of the *original* '76.

On the Fourth of July each year the grounds and parks around the Washington Monument are usually filled with people of the Nation's capital, who come in the afternoon to picnic, play catch, and sit in the sun, and stay to watch the fireworks display in the evening. On that afternoon in 1970, the grounds were preempted for a TV spectacular. Friends and supporters of the President had enlisted comedians, singers, and other celebrities for a show to celebrate Honor America Day.

One of the participants was the Reverend Billy Graham, who was also interviewed on a television program in which he was asked about his wearing a little enamel American flag in his lapel, as President Nixon does. He laughed and told a story about a lady who came to church every Sunday and always fell asleep; and when she was asked why she came at all, she said, "To show which side I'm on."

There always have to be a couple of last straws, however slight, that break the already-burdened back or snap the already-thin patience. I don't know why a President of the United States should feel a need to wear an American flag in his lapel—not, I hope, to show which side he's on. And however well-meaning the participants, I don't want another "Honor America Day."

Honor America Day indeed! The 4th of July doesn't need any PR lily-painting. The date means something.

I'll take the old-fashioned Fourth, even with the old-fashioned speeches by old-fashioned politicians, and declare my independence of *prolitics*. Compared to that stuff, plain old politics looks good. ∎

"IS NOTHING SACRED ANY MORE?"

3/23/69

The Arms Game

A SALESMAN who peddled checkerboards and croquet sets used to explain that he was in the game game. The closest thing we have to a national game game is the Arms Game. It is something like Monopoly except that it involves hundreds of billions instead of mere thousands or millions. But it is conducted in the same way, by tossing around play money—or, as it is sometimes called, "public tax funds."

The principal players in the Arms Game are the Government Team (or Pentagon Spenders) and the Manufacturers Team (or Receivers). A special feature of the game, and one that keeps it from being overly competitive, is that the players often exchange positions. Many Pentagon Spenders trade places with Manufacturer Receivers, and vice versa. In this way, all the players can understand and help each other.

The purpose of the game is to see how much play money (or "public tax funds") can be spent. What makes for good fellowship is that the players on both sides are interested in running up the largest possible score. They are both really on the same *team*, or comrades-in-arms game.

As an example of how the game works, the Pentagon Players (who are on the Arms Spending Team) meet with the aerospace manufacturers (who are on the Arms Spending Team but carry different-color briefcases).

The Pentagon Players ask, "What can you give us in the way of a new airplane that'll run into higher costs than the one we're using?" The manufacturers reply, "It'll take us a while to work out something, as we've just ordered some new adding and multiplying machines that haven't arrived yet. But we think for about a million dollars we can build you a gold-plated plane that can't run out of fuel because it operates entirely with rubber bands."

The Pentagon Players look a bit disappointed but are not downcast.

"That sounds pretty good; but we were thinking of something a little higher priced." The Manufacturer Players, after doing some figuring on the back of an envelope, offer a suggestion. "We can install a Coke machine in the cockpit." "You sure that'll be enough to raise the price?" ask the Pentagon Players. "Of course it will," reply the Manufacturer Players. "The Coke machine will require a bigger cockpit and a heavier rubber band. That'll bring it up to, say, one and a half million dollars, give a little or give a little."

The Pentagon Players consult each other and present a final offer. "Make

"OBSERVE CLOSELY, SENATOR, THE CURVE OF THE WING, THE THRUST OF THE ENGINE, THE ROUNDNESS OF THE WHEELS—"
10/14/71

"IT'S THE MULTIPLE HEAD RE-ENTRY PRINCIPLE."
5/11/69

"WHAT DO YOU EXPECT FOR A LOUSY TEN OR TWELVE BILLION BUCKS?"
2/3/70

it an even two million and you've got yourself a deal." After some more figuring, the Manufacturer Players say, "With inflation and everything, we don't think we'll have any trouble running it up to that. And of course that won't include Coke bottles in the machines. We think we can do it for roughly two million dollars, more or more."

The players shake hands all around, and the game is on.

The next step is the delivery of a cardboard model of the plane, which costs an extra $100,000 but gives the Pentagon Players something they can show to visitors and photograph as an example of progress and commitment to the manufacturers.

Some time later comes a full-scale model of the plane. It is made entirely of California redwood, with the rubber band underneath just a little too short, so that it keeps snapping off the holder and pitching the pilot out of the plane. This can be fixed for another $100,000 plus costs, because the price of rubber has since gone up.

With the game now well under way, it is just a matter of time till the prototype is succeeded by six actual planes. There is an extra $5,000,000 increase in the price of each. This is because the manufacturers' original estimates were based on costs per 200,000,000, on the assumption that the Government would want one for every man, woman and child.

The Pentagon Players look over the six planes and say, "Add on an extra $1,000,000 and we'll take the whole batch—schlock, stock, and barrel."

Termites have been discovered in the planes, and it takes a couple of years to get the bugs out. This raises the price an additional $1,000,000 apiece.

By now the plane is completely outdated and work is begun on a new and more expensive model. You will notice that the game does not end when the product is merely unworkable. Planes that don't function properly only offer added reasons for further spending—on airplane glue, safety pins, and mending tape, all of which keep going up in price.

After delivering the six faulty planes, the aircraft company then explains that as a result of having to sit up nights counting its money, it is on the verge of breaking down; and it cannot go on without the support of the government it loves. The Pentagon Players then give the Manufacturer Players a few million dollars more in play money (or "taxpayers' money") to keep them in the game and avoid having to break in new team-mates.

They're off again!

Even the fact that an item may be outmoded is not enough to stop a game. Sometimes it *begins* there. In 1971, the Pentagon, finding that one more aircraft carrier was just what we didn't need, decided to throw a billion dollars into one. The actual name of this carrier has not yet been disclosed to any except a few of us Washingtonians with contacts in high places. It is to be called *The Sitting Duck*. It will be christened with fifty cases of Cold Duck,

**THE INTERGOVERNMENTAL
BALLISTIC BALLOON**

5/11/71

**"DE-ESCALATE? WITHDRAW? NOT
HERE ON THE SPENDING FRONT."**
3/11/69

**"AS WE ROLL OVER YOU, YOU CAN
HELP GREASE THE MACHINE."**
6/26/70

**"ADMIRAL, YOU HAVE BEEN
SUMMONED HERE ON CHARGES
THAT YOU HAVE FAILED TO SPEND
BEYOND THE CALL OF DUTY."**
3/30/72

purchased at only twice what they would cost per bottle over the counter. After the christening, it will take only a few months to repair the bow, which has been badly dented in the process.

Yes, Virginia, there is a billion-dollar aircraft carrier in the works. And the game is now on. Senator Allen Ellender, of Louisiana, who had seen the Arms Game played for many years, estimated that by the time the carrier was fitted with planes and surrounding ships to protect it, the cost would be more like 3½ billions. That was an observer's estimate. The Arms Game players may be able to get into bigger numbers than that.

In the end, it will probably turn out that more ships and planes are needed to protect the ships and planes that will be needed to protect *The Sitting Duck*—just as more men, planes and ships are always needed to protect other men, planes and ships.

You may ask what kind of game it is where the players on both sides seem to share the same interest in running up a score. Well, of course, there are opponents. There is a common misapprehension that the opponents are Russians or Chinese. Those who think that lack an understanding of The Game.

The Russians, as a matter of fact, *help* with The Game. Every so often they dig a few holes in the ground around Moscow, and our players say, "Thanks a lot—now we have an excuse to build sixty new missile silos. And don't hesitate to let us know anytime *we* can dig some holes in the ground for *you* to photograph."

But they are not the real opponents.

There is also a good amount of intramural competition among the service branches to see who can make the most expensive version of similar items. The Army, Marines and Air Force will all develop similar types of helicopters or planes to do the same job. This makes The Game more interesting than if a single "Defense Department" developed one working plane for all three.

The working parts of our weapons system may not be interchangeable, but the Pentagon Purchasers and the Manufacturer Sellers often are.

However much rivalry there may be among the branches of service, *they* are not the true opponents either.

In the Arms Game the *real* opponents are not competing services or foreign governments. They are *the people who want to keep down the score.*

There are always some spoilsports who don't care about The Game itself, but who keep thinking in terms of money and value and taxpayers and defense systems that work. These spoilers are the Opposition. Fortunately, dedicated players like the Pentagon Procurers and the Manufacturers know how to deal with this type.

Two examples will do:

The Pentagon employed A. Ernest Fitzgerald as a civilian industrial en-

"HERE'S YOUR BADGE AND BLINDFOLD. AND REMEMBER, THE LAST WATCHMAN WAS FIRED FOR WATCHING."

11/7/69

"THEY ALL SEEM TO HAVE VERTICAL TAKEOFF PRICES."

6/4/71

AIR COVER

5/4/69

"I'D LIKE TO TALK TO THE TOP-KICKBACK."

10/10/69

gineering and cost control expert for the Air Force. He felt that he was supposed to do what his job implied—control costs. He was disturbed by the cost over-runs on defense items; and when a Congressional committee asked, he said that the C-5A cargo planes would run $2 billion over official estimates.

For this work Mr. Fitzgerald was rewarded by being assigned to check costs on a bowling alley in Thailand. He was later fired. Mr. Fitzgerald had, as he later observed, "committed truth." He didn't Play the Game. If he had been wearing braid and brass buttons, he would have been stripped of them and drummed out. As it was, the best the Defense Department could do was to get rid of him, to spread stories that he had leaked classified information (which Secretary of the Air Force Robert C. Seamans was forced to retract) and to accuse him of being, yes, a "penny pincher."

This was little enough for the Defense Department to do to protect the Manufacturer Players—in this case the Lockheed Company.

Lockheed showed that it was equally alert to anyone who threatened the sacred Spender-Receiver relationship when it also discovered an enemy in *its* employ.

Henry Durham, a Lockheed Aircraft production manager, called attention to waste, to falsified reports on planes and prototypes shown to the government, and to poor plane construction which was a hazard to pilots. Lockheed demoted Mr. Durham and then fired him.

Lockheed and the Pentagon proved that they knew how to stand up to enemies within their ranks who put the lives and money of Americans ahead of the Arms Game.

Lockheed's C-5A cargo plane had wing cracks, landing gear that collapsed, malfunctioning electronic and radar equipment, and on at least one occasion had a motor drop off in takeoff. The cost *per plane* went from the estimated $28 million to $60 million, for an over-run that went beyond $2 billion. In appreciation for the production of this remarkable item, which advanced the Arms Game and spending costs without providing a suitable cargo plane, the Nixon Administration conducted a successful drive in Congress to guarantee $250 million in loans to Lockheed; and the Pentagon negotiated a new cost-plus contract to make sure Lockheed got a bigger return, whatever it did.

The Pentagon–Arms Contractors team also has opponents in Congress. An outstanding one is Senator William Proxmire, who had the General Accounting Office check the differences between estimated costs of weapons and actual costs. He found that "45 major military weapons systems will cost the government $35.2 billion more than the original estimates."

In an article describing "Pentagon lemons" he cited the Cheyenne helicopter as a prime example: "During testing two years ago, a main rotor blade chopped the helicopter in half. . . . " He mentioned also the Navy's F11F1,

"I'VE GOT IT, CHIEF—WE'LL SAY THAT WE'VE
DEVELOPED SOME TRULY REMARKABLE
BOMBS."

3/6/70

"THAT'S JUST THE RATE OF CLIMB
OF THE PLANE—THE TOP SECRET
IS OVER HERE."

4/13/71

"SECRETARY LAIRD, MEET
GENERAL LARD."

2/12/70

which "managed to shoot itself down" by flying into its own cannon shells. The Main Battle Tank (MBT-70) was supposed to be a kind of military dream house on treads, which "at $1 million a copy, functions less well than the old M-60." Then there was the F-14 Navy fighter jet, which cost $16 to $20 million a copy—"the performance . . . no better than the improved F-4," but at four times the price.

Later the General Accounting Office found that a total of $116 million in spare parts for the F-111 were bought before they might be needed, and after $9.6 millions' worth had already "been declared excess." It also cost some $56 million in markup to buy the parts from General Dynamics Corporation instead of from subcontractors making the parts.

These are only a few examples of what Pentagon Players and Manufacturer Players showed they could do.

When they really put their warheads together and concentrated, they were also able to come up with nonworking missiles, nonworking torpedoes, and plans for a "submersible rescue vessel" that went down in red ink before it was ever completed. All these helped to run up the score. There was also an actual working submarine which, at the San Francisco dock, proved itself capable of submerging in less than fifty feet of water. The only trouble was that nobody was *trying* to submerge it at the time.

Early in the Vietnam War, there were many complaints about malfunctions in the M-16 rifle. In November 1971, the Connecticut Citizens Action Group, affiliated with Ralph Nader, accused the Colt Firearms Company of having workers cover up defects in the M-16 when government inspectors were present. Their report quoted testimony of plant workers, one of whom said about testing the M-16:

> Every time I fired it, it malfunctioned. . . . I covered once or twice, as instructed by the range master and quality control officers. But three or four times the government agent looked up from his crossword puzzles and caught the malfunction. He and the quality control representative blamed the problems on the magazine, a squashed round, etc. These were not the causes.

People who for years have heard from government officials that criticism of their war policies was abetting the enemy and endangering the lives of our boys over there might ask: How about malfunctioning guns, planes, helicopters, and other weapons? But they do not understand the Arms Game, and do not realize that the Pentagon Players and the Manufacturer Players are all members of a highly patriotic team that keeps money in circulation and runs the flag up the pole every day.

When weapons malfunction, it is probably because their spirits have been broken by criticism of government or management officials. This is the kind of thing that gives weapons great feelings of insecurity and causes breakdowns.

"I DON'T KNOW ANYTHING ABOUT SNOOPING, SENATOR—I'M IN THE SELLING END."

3/31/71

"THE MISSILE MAY NOT BE SO HOT BUT—BOY—WHAT A DELIVERY SYSTEM!"

2/23/69

"AND NOW THAT YOU SEE WHAT A LOVELY FELLOW I AM, YOU MUST MEET MY COUSIN MIRV."

6/1/69

"FIND A WAY TO MAKE IT HARMLESS? NOW, WAIT A MINUTE—WE'RE NOT MIRACLE MEN."

8/6/70

To combat that kind of national insecurity, and to insure the success of the Arms Game, the Pentagon spends over $37,000,000 a year on propaganda alone, and this does not include all the junkets and free air trips it provides. The CBS television report "The Selling of the Pentagon" showed how the Pentagon is always on the alert against opponents of the Arms Game, and how it combats them with traveling shows, political propaganda lectures, and films explaining how we are about to be taken over by the Reds. It also makes influential citizens feel a part of The Game by being allowed to get inside a tank, fire a few rounds, and literally get a bang out of our weapons.

It was during the Eisenhower Administration, with its threat of nuclear "massive retaliation," that we heard we were getting "more bang for a buck." But lately it seems that Some Other Country may be getting more bang for a ruble.

Michael Getler, writing in *The Washington Post,* quoted a speech by Vice President Agnew associating Democratic Presidential candidates who would cut arms spending with Gus Hall, the U.S. Communist Party secretary. Mr. Getler then quoted some members of Congress that even Mr. Agnew might hesitate to associate with Communism because they are heads of powerful committees—and are not noticeably "dovish" either.

One was John C. Stennis, of Mississippi, Chairman of the Senate Armed Services Committee, who found that the military-industrial team itself is threatening to price the United States right out of an ability to defend itself. Another was George H. Mahon, of Texas, Chairman of the House Appropriations Committee, who said, "The country has every right to expect that the appropriations of $66 billion will provide formidable defense forces. . . . Unlimited resources do not overcome inefficiency and mismanagement. What this country needs is more defense for the dollar, not more dollars for the defense."

Incidentally, for the fiscal year beginning in mid-1972, the Pentagon asked for $83.6 billion in military authorizations. *Excelsior!*

When you get into prosaic matters like how to spend money to give us the best defense, you're getting away from the free-and-easy spirit of purchaser-seller *Fun.* That's just the kind of talk that can spoil the whole game.

Of course, another thing that could spoil the game would be if those missiles and bombs were used, and there were no Pentagon Procurers or Manufacturer Receivers to continue playing.

We almost found out how we'd react if missiles were on the way on February 20, 1971—a day to remember.

At 9:33 A.M. EST a teletype message went out from the Office of Civilian Defense for all TV stations and most radio stations in the U.S. to leave the air after announcing that "This is not a test. This is not a test. . . . A state of national emergency exists." Beginning with the day's code word, "Hatefulness," the message that went clicking across the nation said:

38

"I'D LIKE TO TRADE IN THE WHOLE
THING FOR A GUY WITH A HORSE
AND A COUPLE OF LANTERNS IN
A CHURCH STEEPLE."

2/23/71

"AND OF COURSE YOU'RE STILL NOT
INTERESTED IN FLYING
GRAVY BOATS."

12/19/69

"NOW, ALONG WITH THAT NOZZLE YOU
BOUGHT, YOU'LL NEED A HOSE."

3/12/70

THIS IS AN EMERGENCY ACTION NOTIFICATION (EAN) DIRECTED BY THE PRESI-
DENT. NORMAL BROADCASTING WILL CEASE IMMEDIATELY. ALL STATIONS WILL
BROADCAST EAN MESSAGE ONE PRECEDED BY THE ATTENTION SIGNAL, PER FCC
RULES. ONLY STATIONS HOLDING NDEA MAY STAY ON AIR IN ACCORD WITH
THEIR STATE EBS PLAN.
BROADCAST EAN MESSAGE ONE.
MESSAGE AUTHENTICATOR: HATEFULNESS/HATEFULNESS
20 FEB

What happened was that a man at the American Air Defense Command warning center in Cheyenne Mountain, Colorado, put the wrong tape into the transmitter. Most broadcasting stations didn't get the message, or didn't *see* it. One broadcaster, who *did* read it, simply shut down his station, because "I just couldn't summon the courage to tell everybody there was a national emergency."

We may have been spared a panic only because the emergency alert, like so many other things in our defense set-up, didn't work.

Saved by the non-warning system!

The President said he expected those responsible at NORAD (North American Defense Command) to see that it didn't happen again. "The White House, like everyone else, thought it was unfortunate that the procedural error took place creating the unnecessary concern and confusion that it did."

There was no apparent concern or confusion at the Defense Department, where officials said that the EBS (Emergency Broadcast System) is entirely separate from the government warning system and that the fake alert "did not affect the national defense posture in any way."

Our "defense posture" remained that of an official shoveling out money as usual, come hell, high water, or national alerts. Nothing stops The Game.

As for our own missiles, there are never enough of them, even though we have sufficient numbers to destroy the entire world.

Planes and guns are not the big items in The Game that missiles are; and with missiles it's harder to tell what they *can* do—besides cost more.

To keep The Game going, there always have to be new models, supposedly capable of doing more than the old ones.

The antiballistic missile system was the Great New Thing in 1969. For a mere 4 or 5 or 6 billions we could get in on the ground floor, which we did. From there on, the costs could go straight up—which they did. It was called a "thin ABM" system because it was a thin end of a wedge into the U.S. Treasury.

The costs of such items are based on the selling technique of the optometrist who, when his son joined the firm, explained to him what to say when he sold glasses to a client: " 'That will be fifty dollars.' If the client doesn't wince, you add, 'For the lenses.' And if he *still* doesn't wince, you add, 'Apiece.' "

"IT MAKES A GREAT
BARGAINING CHIP."

6/3/70

"YOU SEE, THE MORE ARMS
WE HAVE, THE MORE WE'LL BE
ABLE TO *DISARM*."

8/22/69

"THE WEAPONS DON'T WORK SO
WELL, BUT THE COSTS ARE
OVER-RUNNING RIGHT
ON SCHEDULE."

6/15/69

"MAN, THIS THING IS MURDER—BUT
ONLY SECOND DEGREE, MIND YOU."

11/13/70

Unlike the cost of a pair of reading glasses, the costs that can be added to a missile system are endless.

The reasons given for the ABM were many, depending on whatever the Game Players could think up. We needed them because the Russians probably had them—or maybe because the Russians *didn't* have them.

And confidentially, it was really to protect us from the Chinese. *Very* confidentially, 600 million of them might descend on us carrying nuclear weapons outfitted with multiple warheads filled with hordes of yellow Ping-Pong balls containing the sayings of Chairman Mao.

This danger seemed to disappear magically after Mr. Nixon visited Peking. Later, the danger from Russia also seemed to diminish, but varied from time to time. When more money was wanted for the Arms Game—which is to say most of the time—the Russians were overtaking us in missiles! But with elections coming up, our alert leaders had seen to it that the Russians were not gaining on us *too much*. And only they could keep the Russians from getting ahead of us.

The clinching argument for the ABM was that it would serve as a "bargaining chip" in negotiations for disarmament. The deployment of the hydra-headed MIRV (the multiple independently-targeted reentry vehicle) was another "bargaining chip" in the Disarmament Game. The only trouble was that, as we kept throwing in more "bargaining chips," the Disarmament Game turned out to look very much like the same old Arms Game.

Indeed, after the 1972 negotiations of arms agreements with Russia, the Administration promptly asked Congress for more money for more arms.

Somehow, with disarmament on the way, a war being "wound down," and "a generation of peace" upon us, arms spending seemed to keep going up.

Whenever it's proposed that we spend a few million more for courts or schools or something of that sort, somebody always quotes a mysterious saying attributed to Lenin predicting that the U.S. will eventually collapse by spending itself to pieces. But those who worry about Gus Hall, Lenin and "the Communists" always seem to make a special exception for people playing the Arms Game.

What is more verifiable than the mysterious Lenin "quote" is that Communists claim capitalist nations operate on war economies. Well, they're wrong about that. It's not necessary to have a war to increase arms spending. The mere fact that *some day* there *could* be a war is enough to keep the Arms Game going constantly upward.

For the statistics supporting the Arms Game, ordinary calculators or sophisticated computers and astronomical formulas are not good enough. It is necessary to go beyond all these to the level of kids in a schoolyard.

"Gentlemen, this top supersecret security meeting has been called because our potential enemy has the power to overkill all of our people a hun-

"FASTER—I THINK IT'S GAINING ON US."

1/12/71

"BY THE WAY, WHAT *ARE* WE DEVELOPING TO PROTECT OUR CITIES?"

4/20/69

"AN' THE KREML-IN'S 'LL GIT YOU EF YOU DON'T—WATCH—OUT!"

4/27/69

"I'M NOT COVERED BY ANY AGREEMENT."

6/14/72

dred million billion trillion times. *Our* overkill system must be able to lick *their* overkill system a hundred million billion trillion *jillion* times deader than they can kill us."

If new weapons can't kill everybody a hundred million billion trillion *jillion* times deader, never mind. *We can spend the money on them anyhow.*

After all, that's The Game. ∎

THE MINI-AND-MAXI ERA

12/18/69

SHADOWED

The Secret Snooperstate

FRANKLIN ROOSEVELT and other leaders of bygone years spoke of "the forgotten man"—a phrase which recent politicians have found sufficiently memorable to re-use, even if the needs of the forgotten man keep slipping their minds.

Nobody is really a forgotten man any more. As a student in a large school, he may be unknown to his teachers; as an employee in a large company, he may be unknown to his bosses; as a big-city dweller, he may be a cipher to his neighbors and invisible to waiters and clerks. Even his relatives may refer to him as Old What's-His-Name. But in the vast national array of dossiers and computers, he is remembered—and probably known from coast to coast.

He's on file forever in the computer banks. He may also be cased, taped, and cross-indexed, complete with all the other personal data: his income, loans, credit, and any brushes with the law—whether guilty or not. In the secret snooperstate his political opinions may be listed as well. Through governmental use of taps and bugs, anyone's voice may be immortalized in any conversation, however private. And you don't have to go to Hollywood to "be in pictures." A man may be just a face in a crowd, but if the crowd is engaged in dissent, however lawful, the face may be one that the government photos never forget.

The material fed into the data machines comes from people who are only human and sometimes make mistakes. The machines, which are only inhuman, turn out errors of their own. But that's the way it goes. Nobody's perfect, as the files tend to show. And for the imperfect snoop who may have a touch of blackmail in his heart, the dossiers are like money in the data bank.

No one is too safe and no job too small for professional snoops. No volume of information is too big to be recorded and distributed. The files and computers of federal and local governments and private organizations mate and spawn new dossiers, much as do blacklists.

The U.S. Civil Service Commission acknowledged in 1970 that, in addition to a Security Investigations Index of 10,250,000 index cards (on personnel investigations), it had a general "security file" of 2,120,000 others. These cards contain "lead information relating to possible questions of suitability involving loyalty and subversive activity." Sources given are "published hearings of Congressional committees, State legislative committees, public

TAPED

1/18/70

"SOME OF THE THINGS YOU HEAR THESE DAYS ARE ABSOLUTELY SHOCKING."

4/23/71

"AND IF THE ATTORNEY GENERAL CONTINUES TO SHOW PROPER DEFERENCE, YOU INTEND TO KEEP HIM ON?"

11/22/70

"I DON'T KNOW IF I WANT TO SEE WHAT'S THERE."

5/6/71

investigative bodies, reports of investigation, publications of subversive organizations, and various other newspapers and periodicals." Your tax dollars
are at work supporting people who may squirrel away any item about you
they may consider unfavorable.

The Commission Chairman reported, "Investigative and intelligence
officials of the various departments and agencies . . . make extensive official
use of the file. . . ."

They all take in each other's dirty laundry lists and pass them around.
The records breed and multiply but never die.

A man taken into custody by the Los Angeles police in 1965 was released after being held for two days when the police could not connect him
with any felony or misdemeanor whatsoever. But his arrest record was
passed on to the FBI, which in turn distributes arrest records and finger-
prints to local police agencies. These records have sometimes gone also to
such private organizations as insurance companies and banks. When the
exonerated man sued to have his arrest expunged from the city and federal
records, it developed that such "criminal" records were easily added to
files, but seldom subtracted. Unlike the cases in "Dragnet," the names are
not changed to protect the innocent—nor are the records, which keep
piling up.

Government eavesdropping has become so widespread that it has
alarmed many legislators. But few have been bold enough to call for a Congressional showdown with the officials who hold the keys to all those electronic Pandora boxes—and who control vast public relations machinery
as well.

The Department of Justice maintains that it has never tapped a Congressman's phone. Perhaps it has felt that if legislators believe themselves
immune from official snoopery they might be less concerned about the 200
million other Americans who are not within the top governing circles. But
such assertions do not reassure Congressmen about their own privacy (or
anyone else's) in what Senator Sam Ervin has called a "dossier society."

Shortly after L. Patrick Gray became head of the FBI, he told newsmen, "None of you guys are going to believe this . . . but there are no dossiers or secret files."

Among those who didn't believe this was columnist Jack Anderson, who
quoted from what he asserted were FBI files marked "Secret." As an example,
he gave "the Jane Fonda file, No. 100-459279," filled with material from FBI
agents "who monitor her performances around the world and submit detailed
reports on her anti-war routines."

Items reported by Anderson included an interesting combination.

On the one hand, the public appearances of public personalities were
cleverly discovered and carefully recorded by sleuths who could easily have
followed such news in the daily papers or on television.

"THERE'S SOMETHING WRONG ABOUT THIS."
2/7/71

"OPEN ADMINISTRATION"
3/19/70

On the other hand, there were "titillating tidbits" about movie stars (accused of nothing and suspected of nothing) which suggest the work of keyhole-peepers. Perhaps the Bureau's "raw files" are aptly named.

Neither the well-known appearances of some show-business dissenters nor the private lives of others would seem to justify the generous public funds which have gone to the FBI and into its new headquarters, the mammoth (and most-expensive-in-the-U.S.) building named after J. Edgar Hoover. Some of the money spent on the inner sanctum might better have been spent on the inner city.

Anderson said the new FBI chief would also find dossiers on almost every black leader in the country. These included material on the opinions, activities and finances of such people as Coretta King, Ralph Abernathy, Floyd Mc-Kissick, James Baldwin, Harry Belafonte, Jesse Jackson, Bayard Rustin, Dick Gregory and Roy Wilkins.

It has long been known that the FBI maintained taps on other prominent blacks, including such "national security" threats as the Rev. Dr. Martin Luther King, Jr., Muhammad Ali and Elijah Muhammad.

Despite a seeming tendency to focus on minority groups, the Department of Justice probably should not be accused of discrimination. It has lately felt entitled to bug or tap anyone without regard to race, color, creed, guilt or innocence.

It has also engaged in general political surveillance. Legislators who appeared at 1971 Earth Day conservation rallies found those meetings attended by FBI agents, whose presence did not seem to be due to an interest in conserving natural resources—or individual rights of privacy and free assembly. Senator Muskie, who addressed one such rally, accused the FBI of spying on forty to sixty such meetings around the nation.

The FBI operated for nearly half a century under the iron rule of its first director, J. Edgar Hoover. New leadership in that bureau should free it from the personal caprices of a man so convinced of his own righteousness and so securely in power that the highest public officials feared to cross him.

But all the power of the agency and its files are still there. It is not reassuring that this material is in the hands of an Administration which also sees danger in dissent and cause for alarm in minority organizations, and feels justified in spying on private citizens.

Agents of the FBI may feel more relaxed under the new regime. But until such agencies are brought under Congressional scrutiny, Americans in and out of government will still feel inhibited even in their private talks.

Telephone conversations in Washington often include some laughing remark addressed to an unseen audience of listeners. Many a true word is spoken in jest. Under a system of government surveillance many a true word is not spoken at all.

Certainly no word of criticism of the Bureau or its Chief came from mem-

"PEOPLE WHO TELL YOU ABOUT US
ARE JUST SPREADING FEAR."
4/18/71

"AND BESIDES, IT MAKES US LOOK
LIKE DAMN FOOLS."
3/26/71

"GOOD THINKING, CHIEF—AND IF
THIS CRIME WAVE GETS ANY
WORSE, I SAY WE SHOULD CALL A
POLICEMAN."
4/15/71

bers of the FBI while Mr. Hoover was its director. Nor was it tolerated by agents who were not above turning in fellow-agents for any lapses in total devotion to the Chief and all his ideas. One agent's downfall was the fact that he spent a night bundling with his fiancée. Other agents, taking graduate courses in colleges, have risen together and walked out of classes when a professor was less than laudatory of the Bureau or any of its methods.

An agent with a fine seven-year record made the mistake of defending the Chief in a manner more reasonable than fulsome. He drafted a letter to rebut a professor who had been critical of the Bureau. But he made the fatal error of conceding the existence of a personality cult and some FBI deficiencies. With his wife critically ill, he was given the choice of moving from New Jersey to the FBI office in Butte, Montana—or "resigning with prejudice." He chose the latter. In effect, he found himself blacklisted from other law-enforcement work. He had been turned in by fellow-agents who had put together his letter from pieces fished out of a wastebasket.

Mr. Hoover's aides were prolific letter writers and statement issuers, who wrote of the Chief as if he were the Sun King. The consistent glorification of a master who ran what might be called a very taut ship reminds one of the old story about the man who wrote home from a wartime prison camp: "The guards are nice, the food is great; it's really delightful here and we are being treated fine. P.S. Meyer was shot yesterday for complaining."

Perhaps one reason crime has marched on has been that in recent years the FBI's No. 1 public enemies seemed to be those guilty of lese majesty.

It was when the Berrigan brothers appeared in public and played hide-and-seek with a mortified FBI that they became really dangerous threats to security—particularly that of the Bureau and its Chief.

But the Ultimate Crime was committed in March 1971 in Media, Pa. Here documents were stolen from an FBI office. Officials burned with embarrassment and anger while portions of the stolen files were distributed from time to time to the press and to organizations concerned with peace and civil liberties.

The Department of Justice denied it engaged in "surveillance of political activists as such," despite quotes from the Media, Pa., FBI files like this:

> Effective immediately, all Black Student Unions and similar organizations, organized to project the demands of black students, which are not presently under investigation, are to be subjects of discreet, preliminary inquiries, limited to established sources and carefully conducted to avoid criticism, to determine the size, aims, purposes, activities, leadership, key activists and extremists' interest and influence in these groups.

One of the most quoted lines in the widely distributed Media, Pa., documents contained an FBI suggestion that continued interviews (with dissenters) "will enhance the paranoia endemic in these circles and will further serve to get the point across, there is an FBI agent behind every mailbox."

OFFENSIVE

2/26/71

HOME FRONT

3/3/71

"KNOW YOUR ENEMY."

12/17/70

"I THINK SOMEBODY'S WATCHING US."

2/19/71

Well, as the man asked the psychiatrist, how about when you think people are following you—and they *are* following you?

In Powelton Village, Pa., people associated with the Quaker-supported American Friends Service Committee (which had received copies of the Media documents) complained of being tailed by FBI agents who followed them on foot, in cars, and in little processions of cars—making their presence as obvious and ominous as possible.

On an ABC television program, "Assault on Privacy," Anne Flitcraft, a girl working on a Friends Committee project, told of how she returned home to find that the FBI agents had broken down her door. By the time she arrived, she said:

> they were all inside and they held me for questioning in the first room of the apartment, wouldn't let me go into the second room of the apartment to see what was going on, and ransacked all my clothes, went through my books, read letters. They left with my typewriter, books, personal writings, notes . . . as well as about a hundred or a hundred and fifty pages of third generation Xerox copies of files from the Media FBI office.

There are some who feel that when this sort of thing is done by law-enforcement officers, it is somehow better—or more legal—than when it is done by men in white sheets or by members of a gang. I think it is considerably more chilling to be the victim of intruders who make one want to call the police—and to find that they *are* the police.

On the same television program on which Miss Flitcraft and other Powelton Village people testified, Frank Reynolds also interviewed Assistant Attorney General Robert Mardian. Mr. Mardian said:

> . . . in attempting to protect society's rights, there's bound to be some infringement on the individual rights. . . . There are times when the individual right has to give way to the public or society's right . . .

This is a refrain we've been hearing more and more from government people who do not believe in or do not understand that the rights guaranteed by the Constitution are designed to limit the powers of government. They exist to protect individuals from the abuses of government. The "society" which these people talk about protecting seems more and more like a secret society.

In 1970, Americans learned that the armed forces were in the surveillance business, and that it was not necessary to have ever answered a roll call to be on their rolls. It turned out that the Army was keeping tabs on civilians, particularly those engaged in political activities. This was apparently based on the idea that anyone who disagreed with official policies—on Vietnam, for example—was a threat to the armed forces.

A former Army intelligence agent informed Senator Sam Ervin that in Illinois alone the military intelligence system kept a close watch on the activities of some 800 people. These included a U.S. Senator, a U.S. Congressman, and a former Governor.

"THIS IS AWFUL—IT'S NOT ONE OF OURS."

6/27/71

"YOU'RE OUR PERMANENT PANELIST."

6/29/71

LIGHT ON THE BEGINNING OF THE TUNNEL

6/15/71

THE RIGHT TO KNOW—1971.

6/17/71

However poor military intelligence might be in war zones, it was not missing any bets in keeping track of civilians at home. If the Pentagon had unleashed some of that snooping talent abroad, perhaps it could have avoided a few fiascos in Vietnam, Laos and Cambodia—and in the U.S. too.

From all this snooping and tailing, you might jump to the conclusion that people in charge of the executive branch of government do not believe in privacy. That would be a mistake. They *do* believe in it—not for private citizens, but for public officials and their policies.

Most of the same government departments that have testily maintained they had the right to keep track of the U.S. citizenry have been most reluctant to let military intelligence officials and civilian policy makers testify before Congressional committees.

One official who appeared before a Congressional committee alarmed about "big brother" practices was Dean Burch, Chairman of the Federal Communications Commission. He said that he saw the tapping of an FCC employee's phone as a "reasonable technique" for checking possible leaks of confidential information. He added, "It did not seem to me that an outsider had any right not to have his calls monitored and his conversations overheard on a committee extension."

A committee headed by Senator Stuart Symington had to dig to provide Americans with information on the CIA-financed "secret war in Laos" which had been no secret to other countries. It also told us about the hiring of non-combat mercenaries from other governments to give the impression of Asian allies in Vietnam—which I called our Rent-An-Ally program. The hiring of these troops had been another official secret—but only to American citizens, who were paying for such Indochina window dressing.

The only piling up of information comparable to the cancerous growth of dossiers on private citizens is the growth of files of government secrets. There are miles of files of classified documents setting up a wall of separation between the people and their government—or information *about* their government.

The Air Force, in probing for possible information leaks in 1971, found that the Rand Corporation alone had over 170,000 secret or top secret documents. There are warehouses literally filled with "classified" material.

It should be noted here that—just as government officials are not opposed to all privacy—they also are not opposed to all leaks of secret or classified information.

In fact, they are responsible for *giving* to members of the press portions of secret documents—those portions which tend to advance their policies or to give their endeavors an aura of success. There is no problem about those leaks. It is the *unplanned* leaks to which they object. These are the ones that bring them into conflict with members of the press who feel their responsibility is not to public officials but to the public.

© 1971 HERBLOCK

NEW FIGURE ON THE AMERICAN SCENE

6/20/71

For sheer quantity, the greatest leak on record came with the publication of articles based on the 47-volume "Pentagon Papers." This brought about a historic confrontation between government and press.

The documents, a "History of U.S. Decision-Making Process in Vietnam Policy," were commissioned by Secretary of Defense Robert S. McNamara in June 1967, and gave a Pentagon record of our diplomatic and military involvement in Vietnam from 1945 to 1968. But the suppression of newspaper articles based on these papers also gave an insight into the Administration which took office in 1969.

The purpose of the papers was, you might say, to find out how the hell it all happened, and to provide some light at the end of a long tunnel of secrecy and stumbling.

The documents first came into the possession of *The New York Times*, which, after a special staff study of them, began publishing articles based on the documents on June 13, 1971.

The next day the Department of Justice asked the *Times* to desist from further publication of this series or face an injunction. The *Times* declined the request, "believing that it is in the interest of the people of this country to be informed of the material contained in this series of articles." On June 15, the Department of Justice, claiming that continued publication of the articles would cause "irreparable injury" to the national defense, secured from the courts a temporary restraining order against further publication of them in the *Times*.

On June 18, *The Washington Post* began publishing stories based on the Pentagon Papers. It also was asked to desist, and it also "respectfully declined." A temporary restraining order was issued after the publication of the first two articles.

On June 22, *The Boston Globe* began publishing Pentagon-papers stories, which *it* "respectfully declined" to stop. Another restraining order was issued. Subsequently, newspapers in St. Louis, Chicago, Los Angeles and elsewhere published additional Pentagon-papers stories. A government bent on suppressing them found more holes in its paper curtain than it could paste shut. For reasons unexplained, it enjoined only one more newspaper, *The St. Louis Post Dispatch*.

The cases of *The New York Times* and *The Washington Post* were decided by the United States Supreme Court on June 30, when a majority upheld the right of newspapers to continue publishing "Pentagon papers." There was, however, more cause for relief than for rousing cheers in the 6–3 decision from which Chief Justice Warren Burger and Justices Harry Blackmun and John M. Harlan dissented.

The government had, after all, imposed prior restraint on the press—for two weeks in the case of *The New York Times* and ten days in the case of *The Washington Post*. And in their nine separate opinions, less than a majority

"FOLLOW THAT CAR — AND THAT ONE
— AND THAT ONE —."

6/23/71

NEW HAND IN THE NEWS ROOM

6/25/71

of the justices gave a ringing affirmation of the freedom of the press rights set forth in the First Amendment.

Further Pentagon documents and stories summarizing them rolled off the news presses and later came out in paperback books—without any noticeable damage to the country or to the security of anyone.

There were some interesting aspects to the case which the Department of Justice had presented as a grave threat to national security. The government had first maintained that nothing from the entire set of volumes could be published without peril to the Republic. Later, when an injunction was sought against *The Washington Post,* Judge Gerhard Gesell asked the government, in secret session, to cite specifically what information in the forty-seven volumes would be most damaging to the United States. The government cited, among other things, the story of a 1966 diplomatic peace move called Operation Marigold. It turned out that this prime example of a disclosure that would be "perilously damaging" to the United States had been written about in books and in the press long before the newspapers received the Pentagon Papers. Another version appeared in President Johnson's book, *The Vantage Point,* which was being printed at the time.

So the really big secret that finally came out was this: not only had the people been kept in the dark about matters of concern to them, not only did members of the federal courts complain they were in the dark about this classified material—the executive department itself was in the dark. *The Officials didn't know.* They just figured it was safest to keep labeling as much material as possible *SECRET,* and to keep the secrecy labels on everything it had. It was "safer" for public officials not to run the risk of letting the people know.

When a panel of the U.S. Court of Appeals voted in favor of a temporary restraining order against *The Washington Post,* Judge J. Skelly Wright had written a dissent in which he said of the executive department:

> . . . it seeks to suppress history solely on the basis of two very vague allegations: (1) that the data has been classified as "top secret," because (2) the data is said to adversely affect our national security.
>
> With the sweep of a rubber stamp labeled "top secret," the executive department seeks to abridge the freedom of the press. It has offered no more. We are asked to turn our backs on the First Amendment simply because certain officials have labeled material as unfit for the American people and the people of the world. Surely, we must demand more. To allow a government to suppress free speech simply through a system of bureaucratic classification would sell our heritage far, far too cheaply.
>
> It is said that it is better to rely on the judgment of our government officials than upon the judgment of private citizens such as the publishers of The Washington Post. Again, that misses the point. The First Amendment is directed against one evil: suppression of the speech of private citizens by government officials. It embodies a healthy distrust of government censorship. More importantly, it embodies a fundamental trust of individual Americans. Any free system of government involves risks. But we in the United

THE WAR AT HOME

6/22/71

"THE GOVERNMENT SAYS
PUBLICATION OF THOSE
DOCUMENTS ON THE WAR CAN
BE INJURIOUS."

6/16/71

"CAN YOU BE SURE THAT
PUBLICATION OF THOSE PAPERS
WON'T SOMEHOW SOME WAY
RESULT IN CASUALTIES?"

7/2/71

States have chosen to rely in the end upon the judgment and true patriotism of all the people, not only of the officials. . . .

It's easy for people in high government positions to think they have a greater "need to know" than we do—and that they can tell what is best for us. They also tend to believe that maintaining their positions and carrying on their policies is best for us. Anything that could embarrass them might endanger their policies and deprive us of their continued wisdom—and that would be bad for us.

This is a tight vicious circle—one that can squeeze to death the idea of democratic government based on an informed public. The wielding of more and more "classified" rubber stamps tends to make rubber stamps of legislators, and of the people they represent.

The continued prying into the lives of the people leaves them with little privacy except in the voting booth. The public can only hope that by using this last citadel of privacy they can regain control of a government that is trying to control them. By rotating government officials, the opening and closing of doors might let in some fresh air.

There is something awfully wrong when the government claims the right to poke into the private lives of its citizens and asserts that the public's knowledge of what its government is doing is an invasion of government privacy.

It's not a private government. It's *our* government. Officials who don't think so should be replaced by others who will make it possible for them—and all of us—to become once more private citizens. ▪

THE ALL-PURPOSE COVER
6/27/69

"POOR CHAP—HE WAS JUST DECLASSIFYING A PAPER WHEN A NEW BATCH DROPPED ON HIM."

8/6/71

"NATIONAL SECURITY" BLANKET
6/9/70

"DON'T MENTION ANYTHING ABOUT LAOS—WE HAVEN'T TOLD HIM MUCH ABOUT THAT."
12/30/69

"OH, YOU WOULDN'T BE INTERESTED IN THE OTHERS."
7/9/71

"YOU HAVE JUST HEARD A SPEECH BY THE PRESIDENT OF THE UNITED STATES . . ."

11/16/69

Press Section

NEWSPAPER PEOPLE get used to the slings and arrows of outraged readers. Each of them is held responsible not only for his own work but for reporting and commentary on other pages, for mistakes in crossword puzzles, and for pitching errors of delivery boys who do not toss each paper squarely over the welcome mat.

Most of them learn to take all this philosophically. They even get used to complaints about stories that appear in some *other* newspaper—and about shortcomings of "the press" in general. They have long expressed their own criticisms of "the press," which is not exactly a single entity like a political Administration.

Those of us who criticize public officials do not expect them to like our comments as much as those put out by their press secretaries. And we are not surprised when some politicians take potshots at us.

Where things begin to get rough is when it's suggested that there's something wrong or unpatriotic about criticism of officials and policies, and that the press should mind its own business. Keeping an eye on government *is* our business. That's why the founders set up a free press—to serve, in our system of checks and balances, as a check on all government.

Every President has had his problems with the press—and vice versa. John F. Kennedy and Lyndon B. Johnson were both unhappy enough, at times, to phone complaints to writers and editors. During the Kennedy Administration the White House canceled its subscription to *The New York Herald Tribune*.

The Nixon Administration's opposition to the media has not been merely the occasional angry outburst, but a "game plan" involving end runs around the press and efforts to block out commentary that might tackle its shortcomings.

To an unprecedented extent it has systematically attempted not only to "make news" but to make the media serve as conduits for official policy, and to curb television analysis and criticism.

In *The Selling of the President*, Joe McGinnis detailed the successful 1968 campaign press strategy. The working press was efficiently provided with such things as transcripts and travel accommodations. But it was excluded from the televised appearances where the candidate made his pitch to a wider audience, through staged performances in which he gave prepared answers to planted questions.

Once in power it was easy to carry the same strategy further. The White House press quarters were expanded to make the media people, as a doctor might say about a terminal patient, as comfortable as possible.

But the number of scheduled open press conferences dwindled to near zero, while the Presidential use of television zoomed to new highs. CBS President Frank Stanton noted, after the first year and a half of the Nixon Administration, that this President had "appeared on network prime-time television as many times as Presidents Eisenhower, Kennedy and Johnson combined during their first eighteen months in office."

By early May 1972, President Nixon had taken over the networks twenty-nine times for what were billed as "major" pronouncements alone.

Franklin Roosevelt usually held press conferences twice a week. President Truman held them weekly. When President Eisenhower had them less frequently, the newspapers grumbled editorially, much as they liked Ike. President Kennedy held them about once every two weeks—most of them in the State Department auditorium to accommodate more members of the press than ever.

President Johnson tried different formats, including sessions that amounted to trotting races around the White House grounds, where one reporter might ask a question and a fleeter one pick up the answer. These were open press conferences in only one sense—they took place in the open air.

"Quickie" news conferences, intimate interviews and staged TV presentations cannot substitute for regularly scheduled White House press conferences. These are the only means for questioning the Head Man about events as they occur. Even at full-dress press conferences, attended by knowledgeable correspondents, it can be difficult to cover all subjects or to elicit satisfactory answers. The President is completely in charge and can choose which reporters he will recognize—often those who will serve up easy questions that have all the zing of a query to the Bayer Man in an aspirin commercial. On tougher questions, he can filibuster, stall or use them as springboards for political speeches—then quickly turn to another correspondent, who will introduce a different subject.

Still, they can produce interesting results. At one of President Nixon's rare White House press conferences, on June 1, 1971, a reporter asked about the thousands of "Mayday" arrests and detentions in Washington, D. C. The President stoutly defended them, complimenting the police on their fine example of firmness and restraint against "vandals, hoodlums, and lawbreakers."

Shortly afterward, a reporter returned to the Mayday mass arrests to ask if the suspension of constitutional rights was justified. Mr. Nixon again complimented the police on their patience and "minimum use of force."

He then called on another reporter who asked why, if the people had been lawfully arrested, the courts were letting them out? Mr. Nixon felt that since most of those arrested were released, this showed that justice was being served. The President looked around and nodded to *another* reporter, who pointed out that the courts were releasing the people on grounds that they had not been properly arrested. Mr. Nixon again doggedly praised the police actions, which he held to be a model for other cities.

This unaccustomed persistence of individual correspondents in pursuing an important but glossed-over issue made that White House press conference an outstanding one—and the last one for a long time.

John Chancellor, on NBC News in June 1972, noted that "As of June 1 . . . the President had not held an announced-in-advance televised news conference for an entire year . . . the longest period since television began covering the White House 20-odd years ago."

At a much earlier press conference, when Nixon was asked why he had held so few, he said:

> I try to have press conferences when I think there is a public interest— not just a press interest or my interest, but a public interest in having them. . . .

Here Mr. Nixon neatly separates "public interest" from "press interest." The press, and the public served by it, has just been outvoted by the President, who—without regard to his own political interest, of course—will decide what is best for everybody.

There is nothing requiring a President to hold press conferences at all. But there is also nothing to prevent a concerned press from running a little box alongside every story put out by a press secretary or "White House spokesman" to inform the people that:

> IT IS NOW
> . . . (MONTHS) . . . (WEEKS)
> SINCE PRESIDENT INSERTNAMEOF
> HAS HELD A SCHEDULED, OPEN
> WHITE HOUSE PRESS CONFERENCE

This would let the reader know the score, and would help him to differentiate between chatty TV appearances and regular open questioning by the Washington press corps.

An example of a long-delayed follow-up question occurred in December 1970, when a reporter asked:

> Mr. President, a year or so ago you told us you thought you ought to have a news conference when there is a public interest. . . . Do you not feel that sufficient public interest has developed to justify a news conference before the four months between the last one and this one tonight?

Mr. Nixon said, in part:

> . . . let me be quite candid as to how I feel about this. . . . My job is, among other things, to inform the American people. One of the ways to inform them

is through a press conference like this. Another way is through making reports to the Nation, as I did on several occasions about the war in Southeast Asia. . . .

After going on to say that he would certainly be open to suggestions from members of the press, he said,

> I would recall to you that one network early this summer decided that it would be necessary to give opposition to the President's policy . . . equal time because he was on television too much. . . . So, consequently, the televised press conferences perhaps should be limited.

But Mr. Nixon was not being "quite candid" in this reply. The question was not one of "equal time" for the opposition.

What actually happened was that CBS had given the Democratic party twenty-five minutes of air time after months of Presidential appearances on TV; and CBS considered giving this modest chance for reply about once every three months.

The Federal Communications Commission, under the chairmanship of Nixon appointee Dean Burch—former chairman of the Republican National Committee—ruled that if a network gave even this little time to the Democrats, it must then give the Republicans equal time to *reply* to this *reply*.

This FCC decision was overruled by a federal court, but not till late

NEW "FAIRNESS DOCTRINE"
7/17/70

1971. By then no network seemed interested in offering any time for reply to Presidential TV appearances, except for reply to his annual State of the Union message.

The same FCC Chairman Burch had a role to play when the Administration opened its full-scale offensive against news broadcasters and TV commentators.

On November 3, 1969, President Nixon delivered an address on the Indochina war, which was distributed in advance to commentators. Following the broadcast, FCC Chairman Burch personally asked the networks for transcripts of all commentaries on it.

On November 13, Vice President Agnew was dispatched to Des Moines, Iowa, to read aloud a speech prepared for him by the White House. This speech let fly at network television and attacked any analysis or even mildly critical review of the Presidential broadcast. A week later he was sent to Montgomery, Alabama, for Phase II—a renewed attack on the media, including newspapers as well as commentators that were not pro-Administration.

Interestingly enough, Administrations which had received really rough treatment from "the press" were less involved in attacks *on* it than Nixon's. Franklin Roosevelt and Harry S Truman were up against a generally hostile press. Adlai Stevenson referred to it as a "one-party press"—meaning predominantly Republican.

"WE FEEL THE PUBLIC IS GETTING ALL THE VIEWS IT NEEDS."
9/25/70

It was and still is.

Ben H. Bagdikian, author of *The Effete Conspiracy and Other Crimes by the Press*, found that in 1968 candidate Richard Nixon was supported by 80 percent of American daily papers which made up 82 percent of daily circulation.

He also found that most papers were conservative in their editorial policies and two thirds of them ran predominantly conservative columnists. Additionally, Mr. Bagdikian looked over 84 published studies of political bias in the news. The studies showed 74 cases of pro-Republican bias in Republican papers, 7 cases of pro-Democratic bias in Democratic papers, and 3 cases where the news bias contradicted the editorial position.

Comparing the press with votes of members of Congress, Mr. Bagdikian found the newspapers more conservative than the Congressmen from the same areas.

There was a conservative majority of the press, but it was by no means a "silent majority."

The Nixon Administration attack on the media was a "preventive strike," or "first strike," to nullify criticism by a definite minority of the press. It began less than nine months after Inauguration Day, when press criticism was modest and television commentary was, as usual, quite mild.

But there is always waiting to be triggered a barrage of complaining letters and phone calls to the media—which can't please everyone and wouldn't be serving the public interest if they tried.

Since relatively few people are in a position to air their opinions in public forums, there are always going to be frustrated readers and viewers. A subscriber who reads a column or a news story he doesn't like is unhappy. If, in addition, his letter to the editor is not printed, he may be ready to believe in a press conspiracy.

As for television—who is satisfied with all the programs, much less the news and opinion presented? And the commercials! Have you ever watched a good movie chopped up by an increasing succession of ads for patent-medicines, used-car dealers and deodorants?

The Agnew-delivered speech urging viewers to complain to the broadcasters got predictable results. But the TV studio switchboards also lit up with complaints *against* the Agnew broadcast, when it preempted other programs.

The techniques used in these speeches recalled the days of McCarthyism and what was, supposedly, "the old Nixon." The principal difference was that Agnew looked more imposing than Joe McCarthy, and gave the appearance of stolid earnestness. And instead of improvising and smirking, he concentrated on following the carefully constructed texts he was assigned to deliver. The moving finger read, and having read, moved on. . . .

Like the press—which had reported all of McCarthy's charges because they felt this was being "objective"—the networks carried the Agnew offensive against television in full, under the misapprehension that they were showing how "fair" they were. There was, in fact, nothing fair about these attacks on broadcasters and public figures who were considered insufficiently pro-Administration. It also was not fair to the listeners to serve up such stuff without alerting them to its toxic content.

Another point of comparison is that these attacks, like those of McCarthy, employed the multiple-misrepresentation technique. This involved a booby-trap wiring together of some visible facts and quotes from respected people, connected to half-truths, irrelevancies, and innuendoes. Such a tangle could not be exposed and dismantled quickly.

But the main feature of the old McCarthy-Nixon technique involves seizing upon a ready-made concern, fear or resentment, and—with a quick twist—diverting it to the desired political end. The trick here is to get the audience nodding approval, and then keep them expressing assent while you bring out the lynching rope. Like this:

(a) More countries are Communist now than before World War II. (*True.*) (b) We don't want Communism. (*Right.*) (c) So we must go after those Democrats in Washington who have given away Eastern Europe and China and now want to turn over the U.S. to the Communists. (*Hang them! Hang them!*)

With the media, it went like this:

(a) You're not satisfied with all the news and views you're getting on TV and in the Press. (*Right.*) (b) Nobody elected those commentators and editors, did they? (*No!*) (c) So let's support our elected officials by stopping those analysts and critics. (*Stop them! Stop them!*)

This was the real thrust of the Agnew speeches—the trouble with the media was that some of them engaged in criticism of the Administration.

In other words, the press could show how "responsible" it was by abandoning its prime responsibility and shutting up.

The Nixon-Agnew speeches repeatedly stressed that the media "built up" what was actually a tiny minority of demonstrators and militants. But it was these same politicians who, in trying to whip up the voters or gain new governmental powers, constantly emphasized the threats from militants and dissidents—which they called "kooks," "bums," "societal misfits," "rotten apples," "revolutionists"!

So, if the media were "building up" a tiny minority, they were doing so largely by quoting the repeated statements of the nation's highest officials—who kept harping on those demonstrators and militants as if they represented a grave threat to the nation.

The broadcasters and newspapers solemnly discussed the Agnew speeches as if they were a serious study of the media, but never properly dissected them to show how they were constructed.

For example:

One of the lines that got the most attention referred to "instant analysis" by TV commentators who discussed the President's speech. Instant analysis by experienced newsmen is not always difficult, especially when a speech offers nothing substantially new. And however long it takes a hen to produce an egg, it doesn't take long for the man who cracks it open to tell if it's bad. What made the Agnew comment not only irrelevant but totally false was the fact that TV commentators had received an advance text of the Nixon speech —and a briefing on it by no less a man than Henry Kissinger.

Speaking of the "television news medium," Agnew said that "nowhere in our system are there fewer checks on vast power." But later in the same speech, while waving a club at the broadcasters, he mentioned that they are "licensed by government." It is this licensing which gives the government the power of life or death over the broadcast media.

Agnew compared Nixon's November TV talk on Vietnam with Churchill's rallying of "public opinion to stay the course against Hitler's Germany"— a comparison which needs no comment. He followed this with a lengthy McCarthyesque attack upon Averell Harriman, of whom Churchill had said: "He is a man who has a complete grasp of the whole world scene and a man of the highest personal capacity."

Further on, Agnew recited the line, "But as to whether or not the net-

"GOSH, WHAT IF THEY SHOULD TAKE US UP ON THAT?"

3/1/70

works have abused the power they enjoy, let us call as our first witnesses Vice President Humphrey and the City of Chicago." But nowhere are Mr. Humphrey or "the City of Chicago" quoted. What followed were accounts of the Chicago convention, by others, but not by Humphrey.

Humphrey called this speech a "calculated attack" on the right of dissent and on the news media. Following this came the second Agnew speech on the media, in which he assailed Humphrey, who had presumed to speak for himself.

There also followed what purported to be statements by critics of the Administration who somehow were never named, so that no one could check the accuracy or context of the quotes.

All this was not without its humorous side. It was no secret that while White House speechwriters prepared the Agnew addresses, some TV-show gagmen contributed little "funnies" which he read when (laughter) seemed called for. But it's hard to escape the impression that the "Laugh-In" crew didn't have a hand in some of the more serious efforts. Consider, for example, Agnew giving a straight-faced summary of his attack on broadcast commentators as the exercise of "my right to dissent."

What was it that the Vice President (and representative of a "silent majority") was dissenting from? Why, from the tiny minority of dissenters. And who was it that was exercising his "right under the First Amendment"

"UNITY – UNDERSTANDING – MUTUAL RESPECT –"

11/14/69

"SPEAKING FOR THE GREAT SILENT MAJORITY –"

11/18/69

which was written to protect dissenters from government authority? Why, the second highest official in the government.

The same speech contained a boffo finish that must have had Murray Chotiner and other White House strategists rolling on the floor. The Vice President—selected to represent the "Southern strategy," spotlighted and surrounded by cameras and banks of microphones and all the powers of government—quoted from minority-protestor-abolitionist William Lloyd Garrison, ". . . *I will be heard!*"

With broadcasters and press falling over themselves to record and present to the nation every word of abuse and threat that came from behind the Vice Presidential Seal, it was a little bit as if Attila the Hun had declared, "I'm tired of being pushed around."

Never were official speeches so carefully prepared to make the overdogs in control of the government (and supported by most of the press) appear to be poor put-upon underdogs who wanted only a chance to be heard.

The political leaders knew a good thing when they had one going, and the topsy-turvy Through-the-Looking-Glass quality of the situation was carried even further. The Administration, which had practically eliminated open public press conferences by high officials, had Mr. Agnew later suggest that news commentators submit to questions by representatives of government.

If George Orwell were still writing, he might well wish he'd thought of that.

As a final example of the Agnew-speech techniques: the original attack on television contained quotes from such respectable people as Walter Lippmann, Justice Byron White, Fred Friendly, James Reston, and the late Judge Learned Hand—but with little twists.

Judge Learned Hand is quoted as saying that "right conclusions are more likely to be gathered out of a multitude of tongues than through any kind of authoritative selection." The little twist here is that Judge Hand spoke for diversity of ideas free of government control. Agnew spoke for silencing those tongues that did not wag in unison with the government.

Again and again the point was made that critics and commentators were "elected by nobody" and that they must be "made more responsive to the views of the nation."

The idea here is that once a group comes to power through election, from then on *it* will do all the speaking for the people; *it* will decide what's best for them, and those who disagree should be silent. Under such a winner-take-all formula, a party once established in office might remain in office indefinitely.

A diversity of viewpoints is essential to our form of government. A press dependent on appointment or on election by anyone would not be free.

In its attempts to press its own views, the Administration even muscled in on the nighttime talk shows. During Congressional debate over the supersonic transport, the White House leaned on a TV network and the producers of the Dick Cavett show to put on his program an advocate of the SST.

The same centralized Administration in Washington, eager to use network time to pound home its policies to the widest possible audience, urged "decentralization" of the media for comment on those policies. In 1969, Frank Shakespeare actually suggested that comment on Presidential speeches be made by local newscasters rather than the highly trained network commentators.

The "decentralization" strategy became a hot issue in 1972 when Clay T. Whitehead, President Nixon's Director of the Office of Telecommunications Policy, argued against national noncommercial broadcasting which would comprise a "fourth network." He proposed curbing the Corporation for Public Broadcasting, which creates national programs for educational channel stations. These have included "Sesame Street," "The Great American Dream Machine," live coverage of Congressional hearings and a number of other excellent public affairs programs.

Speaking for the President, Whitehead opposed public-broadcast news and public affairs programs. Since noncommercial television is largely dependent upon government funding, it is particularly sensitive to words from Washington. Said Whitehead:

> There are I think, serious questions of principle as to whether government funds should be involved when funding public affairs programs, because here you're taking the taxpayers' money and using it to express controversial points of view, which inevitably is going to be opposite to the point of view of many citizens.

Here it's made perfectly clear again that "controversial" opinions on public issues are not in the "public interest."

What is also made clear is that it's all right for hundreds of millions of dollars of the taxpayers' money to be given to government "public relations" people to promote official policies, but it is *not* all right to spend public funds for the expression of divergent views on the noncommercial television channels.

In June 1972, President Nixon vetoed a Public Broadcasting funds appropriation which had been passed overwhelmingly by Congress.

The move to curb public television broadcasting was followed by Administration action against CBS, NBC and ABC television.

The Department of Justice, in April 1972, filed suits against the major television networks, accusing them of monopolizing the production of prime-time entertainment programs. The government sought to bar them from production of such programs, it said, to give viewers the benefits of "free and open competition."

These anti-network suits, initiated by Acting Attorney General Richard Kleindienst, had been rejected by at least three previous Attorneys General,

"WE'RE INTERESTED IN PRIME TIME—YOU KNOW WHAT WE MEAN?"
4/19/72

"OF COURSE YOU CAN HAVE TIME FOR REPLY—WHEN AND IF YOU CAN GET BACK IN POWER."
4/21/71

"FAIR IS FAIR—WE HAVE A LITTLE BOX FOR YOU TOO."
8/26/70

"I'LL TELL YOU EVERYTHING YOU NEED TO KNOW."
7/2/72

including John Mitchell. They were based on circumstances of some twelve to fifteen years before, rendered obsolete not only by changed practices but by FCC decisions. Some network executives noted that if such Department of Justice suits were successful, they would in fact return the networks to advertiser control and the days of the quiz-show scandals.

But however out-of-date the facts, the anti-network suits coincided exactly with criticism of the Department of Justice—and of its acting Attorney General Richard Kleindienst—for failing to press its anti-trust suits against International Telephone and Telegraph. That case resulted in a kind of non-quiz show scandal. The anti-network suits also happened to coincide with the 1972 election campaign.

The Administration, of course, pointed out that the prime-time entertainment productions had nothing to do with news programs.

Less than two weeks later, Patrick J. Buchanan—a White House speechwriter who had helped prepare the Agnew attacks on the media—suggested on a public television broadcast that the Nixon Administration consider anti-trust legislation against the major networks because of their news presentation "monopoly." Mr. Buchanan accused them of "liberal bias," and said that if they continued to "freeze out opposing points of view and opposing information, you're going to find something done in the area of anti-trust action."

The White House replied to questions by saying that Mr. Buchanan had been expressing "his own views"—just as .it had previously been explained that Mr. Agnew was expressing *his* own views, and that the action against the networks only involved entertainment.

Meanwhile, Mr. Agnew broadened his horizons with assaults that also embraced "textbooks of significant circulation" and a "major encyclopedia."

The Administration attacks on the media not only served as a preventive strike but as a kind of air cover for other operations against the press and television.

Through the use of subpoenas and other forms of coercion, the federal government has attempted to impress newsmen into its service as informants. Those who have covered such groups as the Black Panthers have been called upon to testify about these organizations. The government has also sought to obtain reporters' notes, photographs and other unused materials for its own purposes.

Time magazine quoted a newsman as saying half jokingly that "The way things are going, reporters will soon have to preface an interview with the caution, 'You have the right to remain silent and to have a lawyer present. Anything you say may be taken down and used in evidence against you.'"

With so many government intrusions on the press, one might also wonder half jokingly if the Administration would put the FBI onto newsmen it didn't like.

In November 1971, network newsman Daniel Schorr, whose work had

"SEE WHAT YOU CAN GET ON THIS TV GUY—
YEAH, WE'RE CONSIDERING HIM FOR A HIGH
POSITION."

11/12/71

"YOU WANT US TO KEEP ON USING
THAT LINE ABOUT OUR NOT
ADVOCATING CENSORSHIP?"

6/24/71

"SUPPOSE I SAY 'A HIGH
GOVERNMENT OFFICIAL' . . ."

1/7/72

brought complaint from the White House, found that he was, in fact, under FBI investigation. It then developed that this investigation had been ordered by the White House. When *that* came to light, there was an official White House explanation: It had ordered the investigation because it was considering Mr. Schorr for an important government post. What was the post? They couldn't tell at that time. All they could say was that Mr. Schorr was no longer under consideration for the position.

When the attacks on the media began in earnest, late in 1969, Mr. Nixon, Mr. Agnew and other officials said they were not advocating censorship—which, until then, nobody had thought of. They kept explaining *they were not advocating censorship*. After the Pentagon Papers surfaced in 1971, the Administration achieved one of its unprecedented firsts. It succeeded for a time in imposing censorship on the American press.

Most broadcasters insisted they had not been intimidated by the Administration, but several of them gave a pretty good imitation of it. With licenses at stake, this was probably not surprising. Certainly the medium as a whole was at least thrown off balance by the audacity of the Administration offensive.

Some television commentators and executives spoke up.

In October 1969, a month *before* the first Agnew speech, criticism by the Administration had built up to a point where Walter Cronkite delivered an address defending the media. He pointed out that government had no right to call commentators or newsmen to account for their news judgment—and that "ex post facto examination of our judgment is a serious harassment that makes a mockery of press freedom."

Eric Sevareid was another who brought a note of sanity to the situation, by keeping track of the real issues. In an interview, he said of the Agnew speech that "no network newsman would be allowed to use the invectives and epithets Agnew did." Also:

> Agnew, Herbert Klein, the White House director of communications, and a speechwriter named Buchanan, who wrote it, are professional propagandists who accuse us of being propagandists. I feel as though a pail of garbage had been thrown at me. . . .

It was not only commentators like Sevareid who could feel that "garbage" was being tossed at them. Week after week and month after month official propaganda keeps pouring out of the television and radio sets upon the public as speeches "in the national interest."

As for Klein, occupant of the newly created post "Director of Communications," Sevareid recalled that this official propagandist had said: "You in TV should examine yourself or the government will come in." Said the news commentator, "It's incredible. Here is a former newspaper man making a statement like this. Has he never read the Constitution?"

Sevareid asserted that the Agnew attack should not have been carried on all three networks. More than that—he said the three networks should not grant a President air time any time he wants it. "The White House acts as if it had a priority right to it, and it doesn't." Pointing out that what was at issue was not the power of the press but the power of the government, he went on: "When Agnew talks about monopoly, who has a monopoly like the President?"

As for a President commanding time on all three networks at once whenever he chose to speak, Sevareid said: "The people should have a choice."

Exactly!

Some broadcasters have suggested that the choice could easily be provided by having the networks use a rotation system in presenting Presidential speeches.

I would add that the people should not only have a choice of channels but also of views. In England, any speech by a Prime Minister or leader of his party is balanced by one from the opposition. Despite the differences in our governments, there is no reason why here in the United States there shouldn't also be a reply to a broadcast speech by any Administration representative.

I don't mean commentary, like "Yes, Charles, I think we've heard the President give a real speech here; what do you think there in the studio, Bill?" "It certainly did seem to be a speech, Ed—and I wonder if you noticed the way he used his hands to emphasize what he said? I thought that was very interesting."

I mean a *reply*. When a President or other government spokesman appears on a broadcast, the public should not only have a choice of tuning in different programs on other channels; it should also have a choice between the official speech and one to be offered later by someone with a different view. After all, it's the people's government and the people's airwaves.

When the Administration launched its broadsides against the media, many broadcasters, and some newspapers, became so busy defending themselves they lost sight of the fact that the public was suffering not from too much criticism of government but from too little.

The press does not fulfill its function as public watchdog by saying "Thank you, sir," but by speaking up with "How's that again?" or "Come off it" or "Stop thief!" or "What do you mean, we can't say that?" Television, despite licensing and a partisan FCC, can speak up more and talk back more —instead of "balancing" comments on Administration statements with *more* Administration statements.

Our broadcasters could do the kind of job on the new official practitioners of McCarthyism that Ed Murrow did on Joe McCarthy. Today's bully-boys would cry foul but they've been doing that anyhow—while committing fouls. A tough stance by the networks and the press would accomplish what appeasement and play-it-safe policies never accomplish.

If there's going to be censorship, it better come direct from the government, so that everyone can know it. Self-censorship is the worst kind. It serves the censor's purposes without the people being aware that anything has happened, that anything has been lost.

What is needed is not only a defense of the media, but a recognition of the character of the assault and a vigorous effort to turn back the encroachments of government. The media need to regain their rightful initiative.

It's time for them to stop explaining that they have their rights, and to *use* those rights aggressively in their essential public role of holding government to account. ■

AIR SUPREMACY

8/21/70

THE FORMERLY GOOD EARTH
12/31/70

The Goods Life

IF OUR environmental fate is sealed, it will probably be in triple-reinforced packaging. Everything has been carefully contained except pollution and junk. I should not say contained, but containerized.

We should have known we were in trouble when we began to find that the packaging was getting to be more important than the products, and the products more important than the people.

Common nonperishable items are now packaged in imperishable plastic or in enough sealed layers to preserve them in a pyramid. Many items come in such heavy protective coverings that it is hardly possible to get at the product without breaking it, and maybe a couple of fingernails besides. Not only are yours the first human hands to touch the durably encased corkscrew, but the first to be bruised getting *to* it. And these everlasting containers are all added to the bigger-than-ever middens of our civilization.

The packaging is not to protect the product or the consumer but to promote sales. Selling, in and of itself, has become such a thing apart that in some cases it has even eliminated the product. This is one form of American Knowhow which perhaps we should call Nohow. Prime examples have been the popular magazines which offered such a variety of direct-mail low-price offers that subscribers were overwhelmed and bewildered. The advertisements for subscriptions began to outweigh the advertising in the magazines. Eventually they outweighed the magazines themselves, which kept taking on more and more mailing lists till they died of swollen circulations—sometimes with new special-subscription offers living on in the mails after there was nothing left to subscribe to.

While selling-for-the-sake-of-selling was killing off the magazines, production-for-the-sake-of-production was doing in the Hollywood film studios. These studios were great examples of what might be called the Ozymandias syndrome. They poured more and more money into bigger and bigger movie productions until finally they collapsed under their own stage sets.

From observing the products that were likely to break while getting through the packaging, the publications that became so successful they folded, and the large movie studios that escalated their productions into bankruptcy, we might have projected the policy which would have us destroy villages—and countries—in order to save them.

Anything that couldn't be packaged to death or sold to death or produced to death was likely to be liquidated anyhow, on the new-and-improved theory that anything new is improved; anything that works easily and simply can

"GENTLEMEN—THE ANSWER TO
OUR PROBLEMS AND THE FINAL
TRIUMPH OF AMERICAN KNOW-HOW."
4/25/69

"ON A CLEAR DAY YOU CAN SEE
FOREVER."
12/8/70

"THAT'S NOT AN ENEMY ATTACK,
CHILDREN—THOSE ARE FRIENDLY
FELLOW-AMERICANS."
1/16/70

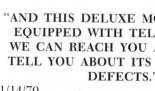

"AND THIS DELUXE MODEL COMES
EQUIPPED WITH TELEPHONE SO
WE CAN REACH YOU AT ONCE TO
TELL YOU ABOUT ITS HAZARDOUS
DEFECTS."
1/14/70

somehow be made complicated; and change is the first law of manufacturing.

It was the observation of these unnatural forces at work that led me to formulate what has become known (well, to a few close friends anyhow) as Block's Law: If it's good, they'll stop making it.

There are many things which they continue to make, *sort of*. In the Old, Old Days, people used to make things for themselves. Later, they were able to get things made by craftsmen; and still later, they got the desired articles at a *store*. Today we are able to go to a similar type *store*, select what we want, pay for it, and be handed a box containing 246 pieces (not counting the last few essential nuts and bolts, which are missing) and a set of directions (which are vague only at the crucial points). Now, through the miracle of modern merchandising, we once more do much of the work of making things ourselves. And we'll continue to do it as long as the manufacturers and re-tailers can count on us to spend our leisure time as their product-assemblers.

A policy of products-and-sales-first naturally results in a policy of people-last. This is nowhere better illustrated than in the field of transportation. Con-sider the airports, most of which have been designed for airplanes but not for people. The airport continues to spread out to accommodate more airplanes but not to accommodate the traveler, who finds himself walking farther and farther—sometimes up stairs and down stairs—to get to the plane. With an insufficient number of people to handle luggage, the airports are filled with travelers weighed down like so many Willy Lomans trudging along to their ends. A few air terminals have escalators and even conveyor belts to trans-port *people* as well as things. And at Dulles Airport in Virginia there are mo-bile lounges which actually take passengers to the plane—seated and reading their papers. This idea proved so sensible and so soft-on-public that it never became widespread.

The problem of luggage-transportation-in-the-airport (as distinguished from waiting-for-luggage, which is something else again) is one that has been easily solved in many air terminals abroad—and no doubt some in the U.S.—where they discovered that in providing man with wings it was not necessary to forget the invention of the wheel. They make available to passengers baggage carts, which are like low-slung models of the familiar grocery carts. These are simple and inexpensive, and the chance of loss is less than at the local supermarket. But they would serve the public. That's why they're not more widely used. You've never seen an airplane pushing a little luggage cart, have you? Of course not. Well, airports are for airplanes.

Arriving late one night from a cross-country flight, and finding no sky-caps anywhere, a group of us saw some porters' baggage carts stacked in a corner. Staring at each other with a wild surmise, we ran toward them—weary passengers ready to throw off our chains. But some airport official had seen to it that the porters' carts were all fastened together by chains we could not throw off.

"AND LEAVE THE HIGHWAYS TO US"
8/1/71

"HOW CAN YOU TELL WHEN
THEY'VE RESUMED WHAT THEY
CALL SERVICE?"
12/11/70

THE OPEN ROAD
7/21/70

"WHEN THE POLLUTION GETS
THICK ENOUGH, YOU'LL HARDLY
NOTICE THEM."
9/23/70

With jumbo jets the airlines have pursued the bigger-must-be-better theory—possibly to the edge of financial disaster. They may also have pushed too far some passengers who find supersize airports bad enough without marching through them to board flying colosseums.

There is no need for much discussion of the railroads, or Amtrackers or whatever they are called now. Most of them long ago made clear their scorn for people as against products, which presumably brought bigger profits. So they pressed on into deficits and asked the government for financial support. They didn't like carrying the public but didn't mind having the public carry them.

The highways—which are not quite the happy ways they used to be—have become the big arteries of surface transportation. They are constructed not so much for people as for the highway lobby—that super-conglomeration of gas-and-oil interests, auto companies, trucking and cement lobbies, rubber companies, gravel and machinery producers, contractors, billboard companies, companies that want to advertise on the billboards . . . and on and on and on, like the highways themselves.

Most people live in urban areas and spend most of their time there. Some are jammed into inadequate subway systems—if they live in cities where they are lucky enough to *have* subways.

They put in a good part of their lives inching along through choked streets and strangling exhaust fumes. They need mass transportation. But the $6-billion-a-year of tax money that goes into the Highway Trust Fund—and the $17-billion-a-year-plus of current annual highway spending—are sacred to the Highway Lobbyists and their programs to "pave the continent" and line their pockets.

As for the public—let 'em eat dust, or hydrocarbons. Many do not live to suffer from pollution-related diseases because they die after impact with hazardous guard-rails which are supposed to *prevent* fatalities.

Meanwhile, back in the smog-plagued cities, the more-crowded buses seem to spew forth more fumes; and the motorist is trapped in traffic jams and parking squeezes. Taxis seem to have become so scarce and the drivers so choosy about their trips that one longs for the good old days when the prospective passenger told the cab driver where he was going—instead of hopefully *asking* him.

The motorcar, which started out as the American dream machine, and is designed to look dreamier than ever, has become something of a nightmare. Its treadmarks record the rise and fall of Progress-as-we-have-known-it.

If there is one product most associated with American Knowhow and The American Way Of Life it is the auto. In earlier days, it was the pride and joy of the American family—and of the nation. Henry Ford was the national Success Story. When politicians held out the hope of two cars in every garage, it was the equivalent of a promise to the faithful of nirvana and six-

**"THEY SAY POLLUTION CONTROL
COULD HURT BUSINESS."**
5/25/71

"NAME YOUR POISON."
7/31/70

GHOST TOWN
3/2/69

**"THIS CALLS FOR A REAL CLEANUP
JOB—A WHOLE NEW SERIES OF ADS
TO IMPROVE OUR IMAGE."**
2/9/69

teen concubines. Today anyone with two cars in a garage is lucky to have that kind of parking space. The two-chickens-in-every-pot, which was the other part of that dream of quantitative bliss, is still but a dream for all the Americans who go to bed hungry today.

With more and more cars came the better and longer roads, which were another source of national pride. It was quite a while before we were taken over by the cars and the roads—or realized that we were being ill-served by the auto-builders and road-builders and monster oil companies who told us about their friendly interest in serving *us*.

The automobile became a combination sales-product and people-package, designed to outdistance ability to pay and the needs of the buyers, who raced their pocketbooks to keep up with the new models and the Joneses.

It was when the small foreign cars first began to be popular that I started to suspect the big brains of our biggest and proudest industry were not hitting on all cylinders. When I made inquiries of People Who Know About Those Things, I was told that small cars were not practical, not right for the American market, and the job of retooling auto plants to make them would be so great that—well it was silly to think of Great American Companies making those doodlebugs. It was no doubt equally silly to think that great Hollywood studios should concern themselves with the kind of good, low-budget films that were coming in from abroad.

Oddly enough, the motor companies did not seem to encounter any massive retooling problems in making each year's models bigger and more expensive than the last, with all kinds of gadgets and—just what we didn't need—long, pointed tailfins.

Eventually the motor manufacturers discovered they could make compact cars after all—though even then it turned out that most of those new smaller models were "bigger on the inside!" and a couple of inches shorter than the conventional models on the outside.

The first automobile anti-pollution device—an under-$10 item to burn fuel more efficiently—was denounced by the motor companies as involving too great an expense. Most subsequent safety and anti-pollution measures have met the same resistance. The motor companies and the oil companies have been as close as autos and gas station pumps, and it's just possible that the gas-and-oil companies don't want their fuel burned more efficiently.

The really rude awakening about our Number One industry came when we began to learn about wheels coming off, brakes locking, steering mechanisms jamming—and all this in the big expensive models as well as in what cartoonist George Lichty described as the modest merely-more-than-you-can-afford cars.

When the motor manufacturers complied with any safety standards, they generally attributed their price jumps to the low-cost safety devices. It was these (and not profits) which were responsible for higher prices. When the

**"WE HAVEN'T NOTICED ANY
BUMPER TROUBLE."**
5/14/71

"A STRANGE CASE, DOCTOR."
7/27/69

8/28/69

**"THIS IS OUTRAGEOUS—I'M
ACCUSTOMED TO BEING GREETED
WITH THE GREATEST CORDIALITY
AND RESPECT—"**
5/7/71

same production geniuses ran into a public demand for environmental reforms, they protested they did not have the technical ability to develop—in
a matter of years—engines that would significantly reduce air pollution. Some
60 percent of this pollution is attributed to our 92 million autos.

It was also beyond much of the motor industry to get back to simple,
inexpensive, old-fashioned bumpers that absorbed bumps. These could be,
and can be, installed at uniform heights to avoid big repair bills.

What the auto-makers did come up with was the super-priced super-col-
lapsible car, with folding grillwork, pop-up hoods and breakaway fenders.
These were designed not only for "planned obsolescence" but for easy de-
structibility and maximum repair costs.

It can be said about these crushable cars that in our mechanized age they
provided a little triumph for human beings. After a pedestrian was struck
by one, as he and the auto were being carted off to their separate resting
places, the man could know he had given the machine as good as it had
given him.

Just as a passing thought—perhaps somebody can explain why, with an
expanding population demanding services, we don't have an equally expanding number of service-and-repair people eager to compete in providing good
service at reasonable costs. Perhaps they have learned from some of the big
manufacturers that this is not "the American way."

When Ralph Nader began his investigation of the auto industry he
started a real "new American revolution." The first mass-produced cars were
useful products that began an American revolution of their own. But the producers of our Number One product, like a ruler too long in power, became
less interested in public needs and more interested in what *they* wanted.

Millions of cars have had to be recalled by auto makers who could not
seem to recall the old American Knowhow.

This was the Time Things Came Apart.

The Number One nation's greatest frustrations and feelings of fallibility
probably came with the world's greatest bombings (by the world's greatest
bombing planes) in Indochina. But these followed the disillusionment and
questioning that came with learning the weaknesses of our Number One
product—the four-wheel dream machine.

From then on we became more accustomed to being less than Number
One in everything. When the formerly almighty U.S. dollar was devalued,
this was accepted with no sense of shock or patriotic humiliation.

If the big car and all the other consumer goods did not make us Number
One, what did? Well, we were probably Number One in health costs, and possibly pollution. We were way out front in possession of handguns and in
shooting fatalities. We ranked surprisingly high in hunger and malnutrition.
But we were far from first in product safety, or the prevention of occupational
health and safety hazards—like black lung and asbestos inhalation. We were

"IT TURNS OUT TO BE MORE HORN
THAN PLENTY."
12/24/70

"DON'T WORRY ABOUT SONIC BOOMS
—WE'LL JUST LET THE CITIES GO
TO PIECES IN THE SAME OLD WAY."
4/3/70

"ONE TUNA, ONE CYCLAMATE SODA—
HOLD THE TUNA, HOLD THE SODA,
HOLD THE DRINKING WATER . . ."
12/27/70

"THE PRODUCT WE ADVERTISED IS
NOT AVAILABLE AT THIS TIME.
HOWEVER, WE ARE SENDING YOU
INSTEAD THIS HANDSOME BUMPER
STICKER FOR THE BIG NEW CAR
YOU WILL WANT TO PURCHASE . . ."
8/27/71

even far from first in prevention of infant mortality, nervous breakdowns, heart trouble and a few other items.

Anyhow, we were indisputably first in advertising. We had endless TV commercials, not only for long shiny cars but for many other things. There were attractive, fresh, outdoorsy commercials for cigarettes—of which we've been among the leading consumers. A pioneer in the campaign to cleanse the airways of these commercials was Senator Robert F. Kennedy, and later Congress did legislate away, as of January 1, 1971, the cigarette-glorifying TV ads.

We were easily first in detergents—and commercials for them—to give us sparkling whiter wash and less-sparkling more-dirty lakes and rivers. With the public consciousness about pollution came the commercials showing how the companies that were doing the polluting were really *anti*-pollution. It is surprising only that they did not capitalize on the oil spills by explaining that the delivery of free oil onto our beaches was part of their cheerful service.

The moon shots, which we watched on our color TV sets, were shots in the arm for pride in our technology. But they served also to emphasize that we all live in the environment of one planet, and that even the oceans in which the astronauts splashed down were becoming polluted. The cliff-hanger trip of the crippled Apollo 13 made us all relieved and glad they returned safely —and reminded us of the value of other human lives. The same moon which our men reached successfully continued to shine down on the same old slums where rats scurried from shadow to shadow.

At the time of the first moon shots, some manufacturers told us (frequently in large tax-deductible ads) how they had contributed to our success in space. But we couldn't be blamed for thinking also about what some of those industrialists were doing *to* us—and to our ecology. We later learned that the U.S. Government, through careless disposal of wastes, was itself one of the polluters.

Eventually, environmentalists became strong enough, and the Number-One-In-Everything syndrome weak enough, that all the mighty jet propulsion of hot air and political push were not able to get the supersonic transport off the ground and onto the public's back. One of the big arguments made for the SST was that it could avoid inflicting shattering sonic booms upon us by flying at lower speeds. Like, see, if you go in hock to buy this 200 mph car, it will also go at 20 mph in city traffic where you'll be using it. And as for the possible environmental damage, how could we know for sure how much damage it would do unless we tried it? The public was not buying it and the Congress did not buy it. More Americans were thinking about making the public interest Number One.

Our vaunted High Standard of Living had turned out to be a Standard of High Living—and even that not shared by all. We were in Number One trouble.

Some political leaders' only previous interest in the environment had

MAN'S REACH

12/26/68

**"IT SAYS HERE WE'RE WINNING
THE SPACE RACE."**

8/24/69

THE NON-RETURNABLE LANDSCAPE
12/4/70

**"ANYONE MAKING ALLOWANCE
FOR OUR DEPLETION?"**

1/24/71

been to ask their aides, "What town am I speaking in today?" But they now became very big on ecology—in their speeches. Yet the same ones who had called for aerospace industry projects that were faster-than-they-were-sound explained later that we couldn't move *too* fast in ecological programs, which could be *expensive*. And we wouldn't want to do anything to create problems for big industries that contributed so much to our country—and to political campaigns. In these campaigns, incidentally, we got a special form of air pollution—the spot political commercial.

One of the most successful of all advertising slogans was "Save the surface and you save all." That was a better idea for varnish than for politics, where we need to get below the surface to unvarnished facts—especially when the political products are billed as constantly improved "new" men every few years. We can improve the political environment by looking for public figures who may not be artfully packaged and advertised but who have a simple, basic design for public service.

Anybody who wants to make things perfectly clear can do more about our rivers and lakes and the—cough—air we breathe.   ■

"YEAH, IT'S A BIG OCEAN—BUT THOSE WERE BIG LAKES TOO."
8/16/70

WHITE HOUSE RUG

4/23/72

Hail to the Office

AFTER George Washington became President, there was debate about the proper title and form of address for one who occupied the newly created high office. Some Senators referred to him with the terms "Highness," "Excellency," and "Elective Highness," according to historian Thomas V. DiBacco, who says, "The American people are really monarchists at heart. Their history is studded with references to the servile deference they have accorded their Presidents. . . ."

In researching that period, he found that a Senate committee actually recommended the title "His Highness, the President of the United States of America and Protector of the Rights of Same." But Senator William Maclay, who had no use for "fooleries, fopperies, fineries and pomp of royal etiquette," insisted that the proper title had already been designated in the Constitution—and that it was sufficient for the leader of a democracy.

The democratic Senator Maclay might be doing American revolutions in his grave if he could know that in time the simple words "President of the United States" would call forth ruffles, flourishes, "Hail To The Chief" (TA-ta te-DAA-da te-DA te-DA te-DAA da) and all the trappings and treatment befitting royalty.

Former White House press secretary George Reedy, in his book *The Twilight of the Presidency,* says that "the presidency has taken on all the regalia of monarchy except ermine robes, a scepter, and a crown." He cites the deference and obsequiousness that go with the office from the moment a man begins to be called "Mr. President." Mr. Reedy finds the aura of infallibility and reverence around a President so thick that he feels "an occasional 'go soak your head' or 'that's stupid' would . . . let in some health-giving fresh air."

We don't have a George Washington in the Presidency any more (or a John Adams in the Vice Presidency), but the position has become more exalted than ever. In our time, the occupants of the White House have been given the attributes of a *Mr. President Superstar,* carrying burdens too great for mortal man.

As for the Unbearable Work Load and Crushing Burdens of the Presidency, longtime correspondent Eddie Folliard noted that he first heard of these things when the country was keeping cool with Coolidge—who spent his afternoons snoozing in the White House. But all that Impossible Burden business has become part of the mythology that goes with the title Mr. President.

11/7/68

"NEXT TIME SEND AHEAD *MY*
RECEPTION COMMITTEE, *MY*
BAND, *MY* TELEVISION CAMERAS,
AND *MY* WHITE HOUSE GUARDS
IN FULL UNIFORM, SALUTING ME."
11/23/71

"NOPE, I'M AFRAID THERE'S NOTHING IN
HERE REQUIRING THE SENATE TO SALUTE
YOU AND SAY 'YES, CHIEF.'"

7/3/70

Four score and seven years after Washington, "Mr. Lincoln" was a good enough form of address for the Chief Executive. But the term Mr. President (TA-ta te-DAA-da . . .) has become so widely used that it came as something of a surprise to hear a correspondent in television interviews use the still-correct form "Mr. Johnson" or "Mr. Nixon."

Correspondents who have appeared on television in those cozy Presidential interviews have found themselves in the position of being guests of the Chief Executive, and caught between seeming to be too servile to press hard questions, or seeming to be pressing so hard as to be disrespectful of The Office.

The burden of Respect For The Office may very well have become heavier than the Burden Of The Office itself.

On that subject I'm probably what would be called a "strict constructionist." My respect for The Office is so great that I believe anyone who is considered for it or who fills it should be held to high standards. It's simply not enough that they keep their hands out of the public till or that they avoid doing hatchet jobs themselves. I expect them to recognize the obligations as well as the power that goes with that position.

The trouble is that the High Place has become surrounded by such fuzzy clouds that nobody knows where the man (or political practitioner) leaves off and The Office begins.

There's such respect for The Office and such a mystique about it that if, some day, some way, Al Scarface should become President, he would automatically be well up on the "most admired" list. Sympathetic columnists would soon observe that President Scarface had grown in the job. It would even be noted that destiny had once more given us The Right Man For The Right Time—a strong organizing genius, and the *only* man who could have brought an end to intimidation by gangsters. Made up for the TV cameras, properly dressed, without a noticeable bulge in his pocket—and standing behind the Presidential seal—he'd look made for The Office.

In speaking of The Office (with the initial letters capitalized even in our thoughts) the accent is on the "awe." The feeling of Respect For The Office is so strong that when President Nixon made a last-minute decision to address the national AFL-CIO convention in 1971, he could be sure that anything less than the full treatment—with a band playing "Hail To The Chief," standing ovations and prolonged applause and cheers—any lack of deference or enthusiasm at all would seem boorish and insulting.

AFL-CIO President George Meany said that *he* thought there was some discourtesy about a President's sitting on an invitation for seven weeks —then suddenly sending word he would come and speak at noon the following day.

At the convention the audience applauded the President many times. Three minutes after Mr. Nixon left the platform, Mr. Meany called the

"WELL, LET'S RUN IT UP
PENNSYLVANIA AVENUE AND SEE
IF ANYBODY SALUTES."
1/30/70

"YOU WERE SAYING THAT YOU
SAW A WESTERN MOVIE
THE OTHER DAY..."
8/5/70

OPENING OF THE GREAT PYRAMID OF AUSTIN
5/21/71

convention to order. But the fact that the President was still lingering in the hall engaging delegates in prolonged greetings when the gavel fell was enough to create public disapproval of the convention's conduct. An opinion poll showed that 64 per cent of the public and 63 per cent of union families disapproved of the reception given the President.

Able, experienced reporters like John Herling found that Mr. Nixon had not been treated rudely at all. James M. Naughton wrote in *The New York Times* that the White House aides had been briefed to make prompt complaints to the press about the "discourtesy to the President" as soon as he left the hall.

The fact that a political leader could arrange such a performance, and then count on public Respect For The Office to support him, gives some idea of how Presidents have come to personify something more than public servants, which they are—and politicians, which they are also.

Even a few decades ago, the aura surrounding the office couldn't be dispelled by photographs of Presidents looking foolish in Indian chief headdresses. There were few who asked what a President was *doing* for the Indians besides posing for pictures with them.

One of the rare times when a President managed to inflate to the bursting point all the awe that goes with the office was when Mr. Nixon dressed the White House guards in those white tunics with gold braid, black belts and highly visible black gun holsters—topped off with hats that were a combination of Early Musical Comedy and Late New Year's Eve. A healthy roar of national laughter promptly blew the hats off the heads of the embarrassed guards—much to their relief.

Anyone inclined to doubt the sovereign status of a President has only to read the 1972 "Anderson papers"—transcripts of top-level White House meetings. In these, Presidential adviser Kissinger brings word even to the inner counselors on what the President wants—somewhat in the manner of one bringing tablets down from a mountain top.

Even more specific is the case of the lawyer-President and his lawyer-Attorney General. Mr. Nixon attacked the Los Angeles newspapers for the play they gave a trial resulting from a particularly gory, shocking and newsworthy crime. He referred to "the coverage of the Charles Manson case when I was in Los Angeles. Front page every day in the papers. It usually got a couple of minutes in the evening news. Here is a man who was guilty, directly or indirectly, of eight murders without reason. . . ." Since the Manson trial was still in progress at that time, such an accusation of guilt would hardly have been made by a fledgling reporter, much less a trained lawyer.

But the most astonishing part of the incident came later when the Attorney General was asked why he had stood by in silence. He said he had recognized President Nixon's error at once but did not say anything at the

1/23/69

"I TOLD HIM I THOUGHT I COULD
SERVE HIM BEST BY SERVING
ALL THE PEOPLE, AND..."

11/27/70

"HOW ABOUT A BOLD MOVE TO
REACH DISSENTERS—LIKE IF WE
WERE TO OPEN DIRECT TALKS
WITH MEMBERS OF OUR
ADMINISTRATION?"

5/21/70

OPEN ADMINISTRATION

6/14/70

time because "It is not the proper posture for anybody to correct the President of the United States."

Even considering that the Presidency over many years has taken on royal status (with the personal effects of recent Chief Executives now being entombed in mausoleum-like libraries), it is not only eyebrow-raising but hair-raising to think that those closest to the President would not speak up to save him from a bad slip. Nothing could better illustrate the absolute power of the President in relation to his associates and subordinates, or their total deference to him. He is monarch of all he surveys in the executive buildings and government departments.

Correspondents have noted that Washington, D.C., is probably the only city in the country with talking buildings. After "background briefings" we will read that "The Pentagon says . . ." or "The State Department says. . . ." But these buildings do not speak without the approval of the white building at 1600 Pennsylvania Avenue. No building gets such instant attention as that one.

It is only recently that many people relaying telephone calls have learned to take in stride the words "long distance calling"—even though the caller might be a crank phoning from forty miles away. But there is still magic and excitement in the words "This is the White House calling." Only an old hand in Washington who might often have heard from talking buildings is likely to ask, "*Who* at the White House is calling?"

When the building itself gets that kind of attention, its occupant can command infinitely more. He can at any time summon newsmen or go on television; he can always be sure of an audience and headlines. Planes, trains, cars, dinners, parades—everything waits on him, and awaits his pleasure.

During a visit by President-elect Kennedy to President Eisenhower, the General gave his successor a small demonstration of what it meant to sit at the desk in the Oval Office. "If you punch this button," he said, "a helicopter will be on the South Lawn in five minutes." He punched the button, and the chopper appeared as if by magic.

If a President wants to get in touch with a Cabinet member, Vice President, Chief of Staff, or anyone under him, he can do that quickly, too. More than that, he can make it unmistakably clear what he wants them to do or say—and what he does *not* want of them.

Whatever permissiveness may exist in some families, there is no such thing in The Official Family. When Secretary of the Interior Walter J. Hickel expressed a view differing from the President's, he was kept in limbo pending the tender of his resignation. When that was not forthcoming, he was finally ushered into The Presence for a conversation which ended with his being fired.

A Vice President who said anything his superior didn't like could linger

PERMISSIVENESS
9/30/70

"AND SOME DAY YOU MIGHT TURN
THE BRUSH OVER TO A
NUMBER-2 MAN OF YOUR OWN."
6/28/70

"NOW, WHEN YOU GET TO THIS CITY
YOU TURN RIGHT AND COME UP
AT THE AUDITORIUM."
10/11/70

on till the end of his term, but it would be immediately clear to everybody that he was in disfavor. No trips, no speeches, no appearances for the President; no seat in the high councils of the Administration; no complimentary words about him from the boss; and no prospect of any Presidential endorsement in the future. He could tune in the television and hear White House statements which would leave no one in doubt about the President's policies—and the Vice President's lack of any part in them.

President Johnson, one of those who filled both offices, said in response to a question in a 1972 interview that "the Vice President is at the mercy of the President. He has no power, no troops."

One-third of all our Presidents were formerly Vice Presidents, and this includes three of our most recent ones. Between 1944 and 1968, four out of five became Presidential nominees. Anyone in that No. 2 position is going to Try Harder to avoid doing anything that might hinder his chance of becoming No. 1.

All this is by way of pointing out that such an official is not just giving "his own views," as the White House press secretaries sometimes tell us. More likely the President and the speechwriters know what the Number Two man is going to say before the Number Two man knows it himself.

At the time of the invasion of Laos, Press Secretary Ron Ziegler said, "The President is aware of what is going on. This is not to say that there is anything going on." However double-talky that may have been about Laos, it's certain that the Top Man is aware of what—if anything—goes on with his subordinates.

When a close White House aide of a President—like H. R. Haldeman—suggests that opponents of the President's war policies are guilty of treason, he is speaking for the President. He would not remain five minutes if he did otherwise.

When the Vice President refers to Senator William Fulbright and Senator Edward Kennedy, to Mayor John Lindsay and to Cyrus Vance as "summertime soldiers" and "sunshine patriots," *he* speaks for the President. If he did not, the President would make it clear instantly; and the incident would never be repeated.

When the Vice President suggests that Averell Harriman sold out Poland (for a gift from Joseph Stalin), he is speaking for his boss—as he does when he calls the Ho Chi Minh Trail "Mr. Harriman's Highway." When the Vice President calls Senator Goodell a political Christine Jorgensen, he speaks for the President. When he links the name of Korean War hero Congressman Paul McCloskey with that of Benedict Arnold (because McCloskey opposes the President's war policy), he is speaking for the President. No Vice President is merely giving "his own views."

When then-Secretary of the Treasury John Connally suggested that Democrats who criticized the President's mining of North Vietnam harbors

**LATEST COMMUNIQUÉ FROM
THE WHITE HOUSE SHELTER**

3/5/70

"THAT'S NICE."

4/4/70

"YES, SIR—WE'LL ISSUE SOME MORE
STATEMENTS ON BOTH SIDES OF
THE QUESTION IMMEDIATELY."

2/22/70

"YOU CAN COME OUT NOW—
IT'S ALL DONE."

2/19/70

were "playing politics with the war" and questioned their commitment to the "best interests of the nation," he too was speaking for the top man.

In every case where officials under the President defame their fellow Americans or practice sly innuendo, they are speaking for one man—The Boss. Whenever two members of an Administration publicly give opposite viewpoints, they also are speaking for The Boss—out of both sides of his mouth. No *public* disagreements are permitted within an Administration unless the Top Man wants different views put out to fog an issue—or to say different things for different voters.

Of course, even a faithful hatchet man can find himself out of a job—for having performed his assignment so well that he is publicly recognized as a hatchet man and needs to be replaced with someone less "controversial." All this is at the pleasure of the reigning Chief Executive.

Monarchs traditionally apply to themselves the word *we*—as in "We are not amused." Some Presidents have been using the term too. But however a Chief Executive may refer to himself, there is no Presidential "we." It's not "they" or "them" that's responsible for the moral tone of government. It's "he" or "him."

The listings of Presidents don't say "Chester Arthur & Associates." They just give the name of the man himself.

Of course, any American boy who can become President has to be a hero to many at the time, and will always have some adherents just because he *made it*. There have even been pieces written in praise of President Franklin Pierce, "Southern strategist" and big-business representative of his day. One organization, with tongue pressed firmly in cheek, dedicates itself to rescuing him "from the obscurity he so richly deserves."

Students attending the Millard Fillmore grade school in Washington, D.C., were asked, at the time of his birthday one year, to read about that President and offer some comments about him. An eleven-year-old said she liked him "because he wasn't biased over slavery. He took both sides."

Some of that same kind of non-bias has been evident lately. Fifteen years after the Supreme Court's landmark desegregation decisions, when the Justices ran out of patience with "all deliberate speed" and demanded action, President Nixon took a stand between the "two extremes" of "those who want instant desegregation and those who want segregation forever." One of his categories of "extremists" would probably have to include those hotspurs of the U.S. Supreme Court who felt that fifteen years of waiting was long enough.

The same "Southern strategy" that dictated such delay on desegregation was also evident in Presidential statements which opposed "forced busing" and helped blow it up into a false issue. As the Supreme Court and many members of the U.S. Senate recognized, millions of children are bused all the time—and have been for years. Where busing has been connected

"YOU ONE OF THOSE EXTREMISTS WHO THINKS IT'S TIME FOR DESEGREGATION?"
10/29/69

"TAKE HEART, MA'AM—AFTER HE GETS IT INFLATED, HE'LL RESCUE YOU FROM IT."
4/12/72

with segregation or integration, the busing *to* segregate was far more extensive than the limited busing to *end* segregation. But you would not know this from White House statements which plucked the word "bus" from a court decision and made it into a monster machine.

When Theodore Roosevelt described the White House as "a bully pulpit," he meant it provided an ideal place to exhort and lead. He probably did not foresee a time when a pulpit would literally be installed in the East Room on Sunday mornings for "church services," to which there would be invited guests and invited preachers—who could be counted on to say nothing disturbing.

T.R., like Woodrow Wilson and others, saw the White House as a place for the exercise of moral leadership—not by invited preachers but by the President.

Nobody gets to the White House without being a politician. The dictionary gives more than one definition of that word:

> 1. One versed in the art or science of government; *esp:* one actively engaged in conducting the business of government. 2. (a) One engaged in party politics as a profession (b) One primarily interested in political offices from selfish or other narrow usu. short-run interests.

Any President is bound to be some of definition 1 and some of definition 2. The trouble comes when definition 2, particularly (b), seems to keep getting ahead of definition 1.

Most elected officials probably want to get re-elected; but there has to be something more important than that. Even in seeking election, it makes a difference if they're leading an effort to end poverty or a campaign to stir prejudices.

Every President wears a "political hat" along with his Chief Of State hat and Head Of The Executive Branch hat, and he wears them all the time. But there's a limit to how much he should talk through his political hat— and how much effort he should devote to passing it around and under the table for campaign contributions.

The White House *is* a "bully pulpit" for setting the moral tone of the government and the nation. It is a position where responsibility should not be ducked. President Truman had a sign on his desk that said, "The buck stops here." President Nixon has said that in the Oval Office there is no place to hide. It could also be said that since the days of President Truman's frank answers to questions, the Oval Office is a place where it has become more difficult to corner a President. In any case, it should not be a place to hide *behind.*

But with all the hoopla about The Office, that's largely what it's become.

Perhaps it would be better if the President simply thought of The Office as a place to work, or as a kind of locker room where national game plans are worked out—and not as something Bigger Than All of Us.

**"COME BACK WHEN YOU CAN REACH
THE CONCLUSIONS WE WANT."**
10/2/70

**"SOMEBODY AROUND HERE HAS BEEN
PUTTING OUT ACCURATE INFORMATION."**
1/6/72

Mr. Johnson (who reminded us that he was the only President we had) and Mr. Nixon (who has kept reminding us that he is the President, and the Commander in Chief, and the holder of The Office) have leaned heavily on that place.

In a 1972 speech about his bombings and shellings of North Vietnam, Mr. Nixon talked about The Office again. All those tons of bombs seemed like an extra load on that Office, but it's been built up to take anything—and everything.

Mr. Nixon said, "In the eighteen countries I have visited as President, I have found great respect for the office of President of the United States."

What people abroad used to respect was the *United States*. It wouldn't have made any difference if the official who represented it was designated President or Prime Minister, or was called Mr. Head Public Servant—a title, incidentally, which would serve as a dandy reminder for a Chief Executive.

I have the uneasy feeling that all the buildup of The Office has somehow been done by ripping off bits and pieces of Congress, the courts, the Constitution, and the rest of our government.

There's something ironic, but not entirely accidental, about a President's emphasis on foreign respect for his office, when people abroad used to respect, admire and envy us because we had a representative government —one with emphasis on equality.

Mr. Nixon said: "I have reason to expect . . . that I shall find the same respect for the Presidency when I visit Moscow." He went on, "I do not know who will be in this office in the years ahead. . . ." But he made it plain that if his Vietnam policy wasn't carried out, "The President of the United States, whoever he is, will not deserve nor receive the respect which is essential. . . ."

I got to wondering, what about the rest of us? What about all us non-Presidents? What about the U.S. of A.?

I haven't been abroad lately. But when I go again—possibly to one of those more-than-eighteen countries visited by President Nixon—I hope they'll feel like giving a friendly welcome to a plain citizen of the United States.

I'd hate to have them open the door a crack, take a look at my U.S. passport, and then push the door shut again, murmuring, "Sorry—we already gave to The Office." ■

©1971 HERBLOCK

"YOU'RE LUCKY I HAPPEN TO BE HERE."

8/17/71

Welfare State

WHEN SOCIAL SECURITY and government projects were first proposed in the thirties, we began hearing alarms about the Welfare State and Creeping Socialism. With emergency New Deal measures to put hungry people to work, we heard about government "boondoggles."

Well, finally it turns out that government *has* been doing too much for many individuals, there *are* make-work boondoggles, and the Welfare State is here—though not quite as predicted.

While most of the welfare talk is about the poor, most of the welfare money has been going to the rich.

The money the U.S. Government gives to the well-to-do in the form of tax benefits, and more direct handouts, runs into huge sums.

A 1972 Congressional report said that direct and indirect subsidies cost the American taxpayer over $63 billion a year, with cash subsidies accounting for $13 billion alone. An estimated 60 percent of all those billions benefit people with incomes above $20,000 a year—especially those who are in the upper-income brackets, although they do not actually pay upper-income taxes.

A report by economists of the Brookings Institution shows that on million-dollar incomes, which are considered to be up there in a 70 percent tax category, only about 32 percent is paid. *Some pay less.*

Wealthy farm owners, maritime-industry businessmen, oil men and others get billions more in direct subsidies. The frosting on the cake is that the lobbying and pressuring for all these big benefits are deductible expenses.

One small-size subsidy item: $200 to $250 million a year goes into "general aviation" subsidies, benefiting poor little owners of private airplanes.

What has crept up on us is socialism-for-socialites and boondoggles-for-big-business. What we have, specifically, is the Welfare-for-the-Wealthy State.

Never in the field of human taxpaying has so much been owed by so many for so few.

Unemployment and malnutrition have been at a high level, though not for the wealthy-on-welfare.

Since 1968 there has been a recession—which only increased the steady flow of government funds to businesses, while the unemployed poor kept looking for jobs.

Throughout a two-year economic "game plan" that didn't score—followed by a freeze and some passing phases—the principal concern of government leaders has been inflation, which ballooned after they came into office. They have frequently blamed this on conditions which they say were set in motion

"THEY DON'T ENTIRELY UNDERSTAND THE WAR AGAINST INFLATION."

3/25/70

"I DON'T KNOW MUCH ABOUT 'WORK ETHIC'—I JUST WISH I COULD GET A JOB."

9/7/71

"SH! DON'T LAUGH TILL AFTER HE LEAVES."

4/14/72

"WILD CRAZY INFLATIONARY KIDS!"

1/20/70

by their predecessors—and there is at least one example to show that this argument is not without some truth.

Those predecessors in the Executive branch and Congress didn't do anything wild like boosting the $8,442 which a postman made after twenty-one years' service. But they did look after our highest officials, including their successors.

Congressmen, for example, went from $30,000 to $42,500 (with the usual added emoluments, of course). The Vice President and Speaker of the House went from $43,000 to $62,500.

Some of the largest increases were for those in Cabinet posts, where salaries rose from $35,000 to $60,000.

The greatest jump was the 100 percent increase for the President—whose annual salary went from $100,000 to $200,000. When President-elect Nixon heard about the increase, he said he didn't need it. But he accepted it.

Secretary of Housing and Urban Development George Romney said (in May 1970) that as his "personal contribution" to fighting inflation, he would henceforth return to the Treasury 25 percent of his salary. He said he was taking this action as an example, "regardless of what anyone else may do."

For this, Secretary Romney could very well have become known as Lonesome George. If he'd made a few more statements like that, he might have found himself with no Cabinet salary at all.

But there was no general movement inside or outside of government for such self-inflicted salary cuts. And there was certainly no cutting in the speeches deploring inflation or deploring welfare—meaning welfare for the poor.

When people with large financial interests are helped by government—to the tune of vast sums—that is not considered help, aid or welfare. It is considered part of our "economic system."

It is only in connection with low-income or no-income people that we hear talk about the need for a "work ethic." This might well be broadened to include those affluent beneficiaries of most of our public funds.

There might also be some mention of a "tax ethic." This could apply, for starters, to the 112 people with incomes of more than $200,000 a year who pay no taxes at all. It could also be extended to the major oil companies. With billions in income, most of them pay a smaller percentage of income in taxes than an average family earning $9,000 a year.

Tax favors to the oil industry, which cost us more than $4 billion annually, do not, of course, include such things as the extra profits to oil companies that result from government import quotas. These cost us another $5 billion or so.

Ronald Reagan and others who pay surprisingly little in taxes assert that their personal incomes and taxes are private matters. But the tax loopholes are public matters. They are also matters of great expense to the public, which does not get to participate much in special tax benefits. More than 37 percent of the nation's corporations pay no Federal income taxes at all.

"SORRY, WE DON'T HAVE ANYTHING IN YOUR SIZE."

8/3/71

HOW TO SUCCEED IN BUSINESS WITHOUT REALLY SUCCEEDING

7/28/71

6/11/71

In our economic system the so-called private sector is largely supported by public funds.

A handout by any other name is still a handout. A make-work program is just that, even when that project is some new super-expensive item to keep higher-salaried people employed—like the supersonic transport.

After all the arguments about the wonders of supersonic travel (for the fewest people) and about national interest, the argument for the SST finally came down to the fact that it would keep people employed. It was a government-business boondoggle.

I'll go along with the President on the need for a real "work ethic"—and I only wish there was work for all the people who would like to practice that ethic. I also agree that our welfare system should be reformed.

We can start by recognizing that corporation executives and other representatives of special interests who receive government handouts and special tax benefits are welfare recipients.

They are like the poor family that the child movie star wrote about in a story for her school class: "Once upon a time there was a family that was very, very poor. Their maid was poor; their cook was poor; their butler was poor; their chauffeur was poor; their gardener was poor. . . ."

Such welfare beneficiaries don't need to go on meeting with high government officials to discuss money. They can take their places in line at public welfare offices, fill out all necessary forms, answer all personal questions about themselves and take physical exams to see if they can do an able-bodied person's work.

In some areas, there have existed "man-in-the-house" rules to make sure that a woman with children could not receive welfare if there was an unemployed man in the house. This was based on the assumption that any man can find work if he *wants* it.

The government, if it wanted to, could be equally strict with the wealthy-on-welfare. Since most of the recipients of government millions are men, there could be a lady-in-the-house rule to make sure there is no unemployed lady around.

Let's face it. A lot of the wealthy-on-welfare have color television sets—and they go right on breeding and having kids who will be a burden on the government later.

In cutting off the millions in welfare-for-the-wealthy, I wouldn't leave them without some job training.

Take, for example, the men who ran Lockheed Corp. into the ground. Many of their planes didn't work. They couldn't seem to figure costs with a computer, a school slate or an abacus. After all the government funds paid to them, they ended up needing a direct handout that wasn't even disguised in the usual big-business way. This was supposed to prevent unemployment of their workers—and of the management executives too.

Instead of giving those executives a handout, I'd have seen that they were

"UNCOUTH LITTLE BEGGARS!"
6/25/70

THE HARVESTERS
7/28/70

"ONE QUESTION, PLEASE — IF IT'S SO
GOOD, WHY DOESN'T HE PAY FOR
IT HIMSELF?"

6/12/70

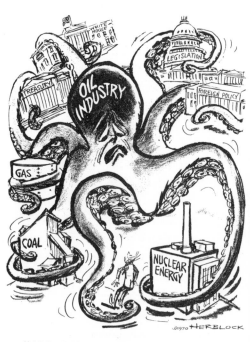

"ALL I WANT IS JUST ALL THE
POWER THERE IS."
9/11/70

provided with some kind of intermediate jobs or training while they were out of work. They could have received schooling in simple mathematics. They could have learned to make rugs, calculate the price of them and become self-supporting.

I'd go even further than that. Without spending even a fraction of the cost of the present welfare-for-the-wealthy program, I'd provide them with a minimum income of, say, three or four thousand dollars a year. This would keep them in cigars, even if there wouldn't be much left over for political campaign contributions.

But while we are waiting for reform of tax benefits and other government handouts to the wealthy, there is still the problem of the unemployed poor. As an immediate step, we can provide them with "workfare" on public projects.

Many government officials who don't mind putting billions into the hands of the wealthy, and who complain about the poor who are "welfare recipients," roll their eyes and express horror at such employment.

Programs like that, they tell us, would take us back to the leaf-raking projects of New Deal days. That's worth thinking about a minute.

In the first place, there is plenty of work to be done creating new housing and mass transit systems, rebuilding our cities and regaining our lakes and streams. After years of neglect and decay, there are all kinds of useful projects on which unemployed people could be working. If we started spending money at home on schools, slum clearance, health facilities and recreational areas, we could work for a generation without catching up to where we ought to be.

These, and not leaf-raking, are among the many things that have been recommended.

But never mind them. Never mind also that the New Deal projects now spoken of so scornfully included conservation work, bridges, dams, rural electrification, construction of public buildings and aid to the arts.

Let's take the horrible example of leaf-raking—and maybe throw in also some of the New Deal tree-planting, which was far better than the timber mining by which big interests are now allowed to deplete great stands of public forests.

Is it better for people to be employed on a make-work SST program that serves no useful purpose and pollutes the environment? In a choice, I'd have to come down on the side of leaf-raking and tree-planting—or even leaf-raking alone. It would employ more people who need work; it's cleaner; and it doesn't do any harm.

The wealthy-on-welfare could join in this workfare too. They'd find it's better for them than sitting around in offices and government lobbies.

If they're dead set against government work projects, a couple of them can do a little raking in my back yard. Over a drink, while they're resting, they can tell me all their troubles. And I'll tell them about my taxes. ■

MARKET QUOTATIONS

12/24/69

"IT WAS A REALLY GREAT YEAR,
MEN, AND LET'S TRY TO MAKE SURE
WE DON'T HAVE ANOTHER ONE LIKE I'

1/1/71

"WELL, FOLKS, IT LOOKS LIKE ANOTHER
CHANGE IN THE LITTLE OLD GAME PLAN."

7/11/71

"NEW GAME PLAN—SAME BENCH."
9/5/71

"NATURALLY, IT'S A DEEPER
FREEZE FOR SOME THAN FOR
OTHERS."

8/18/71

"I'M STILL IN PHASE ZERO."
10/17/71

"IF THERE'S A PHASE THREE, I
DON'T THINK WE'RE GOING TO
MAKE IT."

6/4/72

"IT'S NOT ALL PROFIT, YOU KNOW
—WE SPEND A LOT ON POLITICAL
CONTRIBUTIONS AND ON
CAMPAIGNS TO PROPAGANDIZE YOU."
3/12/71

"I JUST OPENED IT TO GET
SOME JAM FOR MY
FRIEND STROM."
7/29/70

"NOBODY'S PERFECT."
7/7/71

"I'D BE GLAD IF MY DOLLARS
WOULD JUST SETTLE DOWN TO
FLOATING."
9/2/71

"WELL, WE CAN'T SAY HE DIDN'T
'BRING US TOGETHER.'"
2/16/71

"IT MAKES MY BLOOD BOIL TO SEE
THOSE PEOPLE GETTING
GOVERNMENT HANDOUTS."
7/25/71

NEW PLAY IN THE BIG GAME PLAN
AGAINST THE KIDS
10/8/71

"EVERY LITTLE BIT HELPS."
6/15/72

124

"YOU SEE, THE REASON WE'RE IN INDOCHINA IS TO PROTECT US BOYS IN INDOCHINA."

5/5/70

The War

IT IS COMMONLY SAID of soldiers getting their first taste of battle that they have never before fired a shot in anger. This doesn't literally refer to anger, but simply means that they have never before shot at another human being.

Anger is probably greater among people at home who feel passionately about the war. The anger of soldiers may also be directed toward home, when told they have been let down.

President Nixon, speaking to guests at John Connally's ranch in 1972, had some comments on the Indochina War. He said:

> . . . instead of the critics criticizing brave Americans flying dangerous air missions, hitting military targets in North Vietnam and military targets only, instead of criticizing them trying to prevent a Communist takeover, I think they should direct a little criticism to the Communists who are trying to keep this war going. That is what they ought to be doing.

Certainly most of "the critics" of the war were not criticizing brave Americans on dangerous missions in Indochina. They were criticizing the leaders—and particularly the two Presidents—who had escalated and expanded the war and who had misled them about it.

Mr. Nixon was not standing behind those brave Americans so much as hiding behind them.

Our highest officials were blamed because they could not be believed. They had deceived the people about the prospects for victory, about "incursions," about reconnaissance flights which turned out to be bombing missions, about Vietnamization and the capabilities of the South Vietnamese to "hack it alone." And all the deceptions had to be supported by more deceptions, by more attacks on "critics" and on those in the media who reported the war more accurately than the officials.

One of the deceptions concerned the little-understood "understandings" between our government and Hanoi in 1968. The official rationale for the massive 1972 bombing-and-mining operation against North Vietnam was that it had violated these "understandings" by sending troops across the demilitarized zone.

But the 1972 official declarations were at odds with an account written by Daniel I. Davidson, who was a member of the U.S. delegation which negotiated the 1968 understandings.

These included an agreement by the United States to stop its bombing and naval bombardment north of the DMZ. But, said Mr. Davidson:

ANOTHER SUMMIT

5/3/72

CHOPPER

1/31/71

**"IF YOU COULD WALK WITH THE
DOMINOES, TALK WITH THE DOMINOES . . ."**

7/15/70

In May of 1970, shortly after he had sent American troops into Cambodia, President Nixon in four days sent over 500 planes to raid the North. It was officially described as a "protective reaction" . . .

Another series of heavy American attacks took place a few months later—also officially described as "protective reaction"—but without violations of the understandings by Hanoi. Mr. Nixon decided to understand the understandings to mean what he wanted them to mean. Concluded Mr. Davidson: ". . . the crucial point is that after painstaking negotiations, the word of the United States was given. This Administration had no right to dishonor it. Having done so, for it to charge North Vietnam with violating the understanding is the purest hypocrisy."

Nevertheless, the speeches continued to refer to "national honor," though the reasons for what we did—and for the war itself—kept changing.

We were there in support of treaties or solemn commitments.

We were there to protect our men who were already there.

We were there to defend our vital interests.

We were there because Southeast Asian countries would fall like dominoes if we were not—and later, because countries all over the world would fall if we did not see the war settled on proper terms.

So we were there to maintain the credibility of American power in the world—although it had long ago become evident that because of the Indochina War, we were less likely to engage in such an undertaking anywhere again.

We were there to show that we were not a "pitiful helpless giant"—though it was obvious that we were pitifully and helplessly bogged down, and apparently in thrall to the Thieu regime.

We were there fighting for the right of the South Vietnamese to determine their own government. Yet we countenanced a one-man "election" which all the world knew to be a farce.

We were there to free our prisoners of war—and constantly sent more pilots on raids which added to the POW lists.

We were there to prevent the expansion of Communist influence by China and Russia—nations whose weapons were helping to kill Americans in Indochina.

After President Nixon visited China and Russia, these countries apparently stopped being ominous threats.

We became friendly enough to welcome touring Chinese parties to the U.S. When one group went through an auto plant in Detroit, reporters noted that some Vietnam war veterans in the plant found this incongruous. "We're shooting them over there and shaking hands with them over here," said one.

We weren't actually shooting Chinese. But you can hardly blame the confused veterans who had been told that the Chinese were the enemy too, supporting the men who were killing our troops.

Well, then, since the big powers weren't the enemies any more, we were

"WHAT DO YOU MEAN, WHAT HAVE WE BEEN
FIGHTING FOR? HERE'S AN EXAMPLE OF A
VIETNAMESE DETERMINING HIS OWN
FUTURE, ALREADY."

9/3/71

"I AM NOT A PITIFUL HELPLESS
GIANT, I AM NOT A PITIFUL
HELPLESS GIANT, I AM NOT A
PITIFUL HELPLESS . . ."

7/23/70

"A VIETNAMESE SOLUTION TO A
VIETNAMESE PROBLEM."
—NIXON ADMINISTRATION OFFICIALS
ON THE THIEU "RE-ELECTION"

10/5/71

fighting to prevent a North Vietnam takeover—which would result in a blood-bath—while dozens of thousands kept dying in a constant bloodbath.

The South Vietnamese were doing so well that we had to throw in the enormous weight of our navy and air force to support them, and we had to mine the harbors of North Vietnam besides.

After January 1969 and "Vietnamization," we dropped a greater tonnage of bombs than had ever been unleashed before—greater than all those dropped during the Johnson Administration, or during all of World War II.

And to what end? To provide our highest officials with a face-saving way out—without regard to all the Indochinese people who would be faceless to us except for the anguish caught in pictures by news photo and television cameramen.

During that same "winding down the war" period, Americans suffered over 105,000 wounded and over 19,000 dead—more than a third of our casualties during the entire war.

The Pentagon has many statistics on the war.

On the basis of its figures about bombs alone, *Washington Post* correspondent George C. Wilson calculated in May 1972 that we had dropped enough bombs and other air ordnance to provide 262 pounds of explosives per person for everybody in North and South Vietnam, Laos and Cambodia.

But most significant are the non-statistics:

The Pentagon does not keep track of civilian casualties in Indochina.

Elaborate figures are reeled off about enemy dead. But the people we've supposedly been protecting have not been counted—and haven't seemed to count to our government.

Officially, all those dead and wounded and homeless are non-persons in a non-personal war.

Our leaders have often said that we do not covet territory. And indeed there was little to covet in much of the land, so pocked with craters and bomb fragments that it was of little use to those who had once made a living on it. Ironically, even that torn and battered land seemed to matter more than its people.

The United States Agency for International Development (AID) has provided some figures on refugees. By mid-1972, the total number of refugees in South Vietnam alone had probably topped 6½ million—more than a third of the entire population.

The U.S. Senate Subcommittee on Refugees estimated that, as of mid-1971, two to three million Cambodians had become refugees—more than a third of the population of that country. About a million more became refugees in Laos. In a little over a year that country suffered 10,000 civilian deaths and 30,000 civilian casualties.

Most of those made homeless and many of those wounded, killed, or barely able to survive were not primarily refugees from enemy attacks but from our bombings.

4/2/71

"THE OTHER SIDE"

11/26/69

"AND I TRUST YOU'LL TAKE AN
EQUALLY CLOSE LOOK AT
COMPLAINTS ABOUT ME."

12/4/69

"HOW WOULD YOU LIKE TO SEE
SOME HOT PICTURES INSTEAD?"

4/4/72

Wise advisers said, when we first intervened in Vietnam, that we would seem to be occidentals fighting Asians. This turned out to be more true than they could have foreseen. Not only our foes but many of our friends in Indochina were uprooted, maimed and killed. The bombs killed impersonally.

Earlier in the war American combat troops killed many South Vietnamese, because Vietnamese friends and foes *did* look alike to them.

Few killed as wantonly as those who took part in the massacres at Mylai and My Khe. Long after those events, Seymour M. Hersh interviewed some of the participants and quoted one who said, "We were out there having a good time. . . . It was sort of like being in a shooting gallery."

Of course these "incidents" were not typical. What was shockingly typical was, as Hersh reported in *Cover-Up,* that the cover-up included officers from bottom to top.

Even the cover-up government investigation of Mylai showed far more killed in the massacre than had been admitted. But that official report was also covered up—until Hersh disclosed details of it in the press.

How could anyone who cared about our moral position and about the people we were helping to defend be satisfied with anything less than the fullest investigation of these massacres? How could a Commander-in-Chief do any less than make it clear that such occurrences were intolerable?

One man, Lieutenant William Calley, was tried and convicted. But more important than the trial of this individual officer was the President's intervention on his behalf and the letter written to President Nixon by the Calley case prosecutor, Captain Aubrey M. Daniels.

Captain Daniels said, in part:

> Certainly, no one wanted to believe what occurred at Mylai, including the officers who sat in judgment of Lieutenant Calley. To believe, however, that any large percentage of the population could believe the evidence which was presented and approve of the conduct of Lieutenant Calley would be as shocking to my conscience as the conduct itself, since I believe that we are still a civilized nation.
>
> If such be the case, then the war in Vietnam has brutalized us more than I care to believe, and it must cease. How shocking it is if so many people across this nation have failed to see the moral issue which was involved in the trial of Lieutenant Calley—that it is unlawful for an American soldier to summarily execute unarmed and unresisting men, women, children and babies.
>
> But how much more appalling it is to see so many of the political leaders of the nation who have failed to see the moral issue or, having seen it, to compromise it for political motive. . . .

Captain Daniels pointed out that respect for the legal process had been weakened, that the image of a convicted murderer as a hero had been enhanced, and that support was given to those who unjustly criticized the six loyal and honorable officers who fulfilled their duty as jurors. He asked:

> Have you considered those men in making your decisions? The men who since rendering their verdict have found themselves and their families

THE OTHER TROOP WITHDRAWALS

11/7/71

FOURTH YEAR OF THE "PLAN TO
END THE WAR" (CONTD.)

5/10/72

"EVERY ONCE IN A WHILE SOME
VICIOUS DIKE OR DAM ATTACKS
OUR PLANES AS THEY'RE FLYING
OVER MILITARY TARGETS."

7/18/72

the subject of vicious attacks upon their honor, integrity and loyalty to this nation.

It would seem to me to be more appropriate for you as the President to have said something in their behalf and to remind the nation of the purpose of our legal system and the respect it should command.

I would expect that the President of the United States, a man whom I believed should and would provide the moral leadership for this nation, would stand fully behind the law of this land on a moral issue which is so clear and about which there can be no compromise.

For this nation to condone the acts of Lieutenant Calley is to make us no better than our enemies and make any pleas by this nation for the humane treatment of our own prisoners meaningless. . . .

Three years after Mylai, a reporter who visited there found the people in that area still afraid—not now afraid of being massacred, but afraid of starvation, as they scrounged the devastated countryside for whatever they could find to eat. These hungry people were living under a corrupt government which was receiving billions of dollars in American aid.

In the order to kill at Mylai, the phrase had been "waste them."

The words apply to the whole war.

All the men, women and children in Indochina who became casualties of the war—wasted. Villages—wasted. Much of Indochina itself—wasted. Over fifty-five thousand American lives—wasted. Much of the energies and treasures of our nation—wasted. Years of progress at home—wasted.

Nothing in our recent history has been so divisive or has so shaken our country as The War—President Johnson's War, which was continued and expanded to become President Nixon's War.

Through both Administrations we had a "credibility gap," which came to embrace everything from circumlocutions to outright official lying. Great numbers of Americans learned to distrust their leaders.

A chasm existed between those who no longer believed in the war and those who followed the official line.

The two views were articulated when Secretary of Defense Melvin Laird appeared before the Senate Foreign Relations Committee after the 1972 bombings of Hanoi and Haiphong began.

Secretary Laird did most of the talking, with Chairman William Fulbright and other committee members occasionally getting in a question. Mr. Laird is an expert filibusterer who merely raises his voice and talks on when committee members try to hold him to questions. Granted that he was putting on a performance for the press and television—still, it was interesting to note the complete gap between the questions of the Senators and what amounted to the speeches by Secretary Laird.

Senator Fulbright, who had patiently told Administration witnesses of his puzzlement about why "this particular piece of real estate" was so important to us, wondered again how the preservation of "the particular form of government of Mr. Thieu" was vital to the security of the United States. About

©1972 HERBLOCK

THE UNSCHEDULED WITHDRAWALS

5/2/72

the pursuit of the war, he asked, "What is the purpose . . .? What is the objective?"

Secretary Laird continued on and on about immediate events, strategy and precise timing of military actions—all the strategic items one might give in a war-room lecture.

Long ago and far away were the Geneva accords providing for an all-Vietnam election which Ho Chi Minh was expected to win, and which Secretary of State John Foster Dulles had determined should not occur. But in Secretary Laird's torrent of words, even the recent past was washed away. Everything began with the current North Vietnamese offensive.

In response to questions about the U.S.-North Vietnam understandings, Secretary Laird simply kept repeating that "they" had violated the understandings. "They" had moved down in a massive invasion. We were stopping the invasion.

It was "we" against "them." As he spoke, he became more fervent, his brows darkened, his eyes gleamed. He seemed to be caught up in his own game. There was no real dialogue between the Secretary and the Senator who did not see how the Thieu Government was worth the tremendous cost and damage to our own country. It was like a man listening to a football game on a transistor radio at a funeral. He was there, but there was no connection.

I thought about the man in *1984*, who, at the very end, still found himself alert and excited at the trumpet blast to announce more victory news on the telescreen—the broken man at his little table in the café who listened raptly and whose feet began to move convulsively under the table—"running, swiftly running with the crowds outside."

As the Secretary made his statements for the Administration, he seemed to hear the trumpet blast of his own words; and I almost wondered if his feet were moving under the table.

Other feet were still running to the patriotic calls about how "we" must triumph over "them."

There were still the trumpet blasts, still the new announcements of bold actions and success. And still unanswered the questions about why we were there, why the 55,000 American dead, the hundreds of thousands of wounded, the ravaged land, the refugees.

So many feet had run for so long. So many feet would never run again.

■

"LET ME KNOW WHEN THERE'S A
WINDING-DOWN."

4/20/72

THE BIG PUSH

7/13/71

"THESE HELICOPTERS ARE
COMPARATIVELY SAFE,
AREN'T THEY?"

3/9/71

"VIETNAMIZATION HAS BEEN
ASTONISHINGLY SUCCESSFUL."

6/7/72   —SECRETARY LAIRD

"OF COURSE WE'RE HITTING NORTH VIETNAMESE CIVILIANS—WHY SHOULD WE TREAT THEM ANY BETTER THAN WE DO THE SOUTH VIETNAMESE?"

5/25/72

"THEY SAY WE HAVE 'SMART BOMBS'—NOW, IF ONLY WE HAD SMART LEADERS."

7/5/72

"THEY JUST DON'T WASH."

5/11/72

WHITE FLAG

7/7/72

138

"THE TROUBLE WITH KIDS TODAY IS THEY HAVE NO RESPECT
FOR OUR INSTITUTIONS."

3/24/70

Battle of Capitol Hill

Whenever I hear some politician attack the papers of the Eastern Press or the Establishment Press, I have an urge to take off after one of those journals too. My complaint is about a supposedly respectable and responsible Eastern Establishment publication which consistently misquotes our public officials and misrepresents what those officials have said and done. I refer to that well-known Washington, D.C., publication, the *Congressional Record*.

No newspaper editor in the country would want to—or dare to—alter statements of public officials and mislead readers as do the five hundred or so members of Congress. They are "editors" who not only revise, but add to, subtract from, remove, insert what was never said or totally change what they *have* said publicly. No other publication would consistently give the impression that speeches were made—when, in fact, they were never spoken at all. More than that, speeches are frequently inserted into the day's *Record* by members who were not even there. On at least one occasion, the *Record* showed a member of Congress delivering eight speeches, on as many subjects, on a day when he was absent.

The *Congressional Record* is not fair to the taxpayers who support it, or to those who look to it for a factual account of what happened in Congress. It is also unfair to members of the press, who may accurately report a dialogue which occurred on the floor of Congress—which readers cannot find anywhere in the supposedly authentic *Record*. This is because the Congressmen who exchanged the words decided to drop them down the memory hole, and perhaps substitute something else. What we frequently get in the *Record* is an almost instantly rewritten history—a remarkable feat of sleight of hand by the Congressmen.*

I don't know whether televising sessions of Congress would help, although it might do wonders for attendance records. But there's no reason why the printed *Record* shouldn't be what its name implies. I'd go along with the proposal that the legislators might still toss in any additional stuff they wanted, so long as the inserted material was run in a different type style or identified in some other way.

As for Congressional *voting* records, we've at least been getting a better account of those than we used to. This is due to a 1970 procedural reform which provided for recorded teller votes in the House of Representatives. These replaced the fast-shuffle votes which had given not much more than the final tally. They had also given many legislators a chance to con voters

---

* Wherever appropriate, the term Congressmen includes women—whose representation in Congress has been all too small.

THE GODFATHER

7/19/70

"MAYBE WE'D BE MORE CONVINCING IF WE COULD BUST OUT OF HERE."

7/5/70

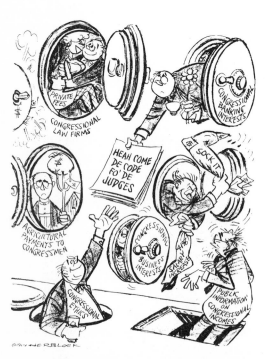

LEGISLATIVE LAUGH-IN

5/28/69

"I SEE WHY THEY TALK ABOUT FRIENDLY FINANCIAL INSTITUTIONS."

8/6/69

with after-the-fact accounts of what they had done—in the manner of W. C. Fields turning the quickly shuffled deck of cards face up and saying, "Why, yes, I'll be glad to show you the ace I held—there it is."

The same 91st Congress also required disclosure of votes taken in closed-committee meetings—although it didn't require the opening up of the meetings themselves. These and a few other reforms were all to the good. But Congress can do with a lot more.

The most needed reform is one that would get off Congress's back that great-granddaddy of all legislative abuses—the old-man-of-the-sea seniority system. This is a system not for operating a representative government but for strangling it. It often make fiefdoms of Congressional committees—fiefdoms in which the people's representatives are subject to the whims of chairmen who have little responsibility to anybody.

One member of Congress points out that in the last twenty years, 88 percent of the House committee chairmen have come from virtually one-party districts. They face little opposition in elections at home, and the seniority system assures them of no opposition for their posts in Congress.

One-man one-vote rulings have helped give us representative government in elections back home. But real representative government ends when it gets to Washington, D.C., where the seniority system takes over.

Government ethics have not done so well in Washington either.

Under the Nixon Administration the ethics of the executive department have become a national scandal. But the ethical standards legislators have set for themselves still need improvement too.

Senator James O. Eastland of Mississippi collected $160,000 a year from the U.S. on farm subsidy payments while sitting on the Senate Agriculture Committee—and that's scandalous. So is the fact that Congressmen who hold bank directorships or other banking interests sit on committees that have to do with banking—and members with oil interests vote in committees having to do with *those* interests.

No member of Congress should vote in decisions on anything in which the Congressman has a personal financial interest. That seems like a minimal ethical reform, even if there would still be logrolling between some special-interest Congressmen.

Mark Twain, with his special mixture of outrage and outrageous exaggeration, wrote, "It would be possible to show by facts and figures that there is no distinctly American criminal class except Congress." These days there is less hyperbole in jokes about our national legislators. Nevertheless, Congress is still something of a perennial fall guy.

This is partly because of procedural methods and partly because of a general impression of legislative babel. There is also another reason. In any hassle with Congress, the President is generally looked on as the national flag-bearer. One man sitting in the Oval Office is regarded as a leader. Five hundred legislators with differing views are a gaggle.

**"DON'T JUST STAND THERE—
DO SOMETHING!"**

9/1/70

1/21/71

**"LISTEN—IF I HEAR ANY MORE
COMPLAINTS, I MAY
STOP HURRYING."**

1/26/71

**"YOU'RE AN OFFICER AND A
GENTLEMAN—AND BOTH OF YOU
ARE VERY GENEROUS."**

4/9/71

So prevalent is the follow-the-leader concept that at the conclusion of a session of Congress, publications often give box scores on how many White House recommendations Congress approved. But that's not a very good standard for judging what was actually accomplished.

Many a Chief Executive has been frustrated in noble efforts by what Woodrow Wilson called "a little group of willful men."

But willful men in the Senate did no more to destroy Wilson's hope of preventing World War II than did willful men in the White House to destroy hopes for an early end to our involvement in the Vietnam war.

Congress does not have a monopoly on "obstructionism." Since 1968, for example, the roadblocks to domestic progress have often been put up at the executive end of Pennsylvania Avenue.

Through many Administrations, worthy executive proposals have been waylaid and laid to rest in Congress. But lately many worthy Congressional bills have come under the ax of the Presidential veto. The difference between Congress and the President is that a President can strike down a bill with a flourish and a ringing statement condemning "extravagance" or "irresponsibility."

These make him seem to be leading, even if he's only leading us back into a quagmire. The assorted members of Congress can't go on television to speak with a single voice or to make a dramatic gesture—even in defense of their constitutional right to vote on making war.

There was a time when legislation in general was supposed to originate in Congress—not in the White House. But today, even though Congress may still take the lead in bringing forth legislation, the White House is likely to take over as its own those measures which prove popular—and to kill others.

It is always easy for a President to send Congress a list of things to do and then blame it for not snapping into action to pass everything. But these executive "laundry lists" can be largely political rhetoric. And sometimes Presidents don't really get in and pitch for their own programs.

Most importantly, there are some White House proposals sent to Congress which it darn well *should* reject—and which never should have been sent to it in the first place.

To say, as Presidents sometimes do, that they have sent to Congress umpty-ump proposals of which it has passed only ump is to give numbers that don't really tell the score. They don't tell us what was important or unimportant, what was good or bad.

It's a little like the comic's version of a sports announcer's rapid-fire closing: "*. . . and-now, folks, for-a-few-quick-last-minute-scores: 32-10, 6-3, 18-12, and how-about-this-one-folks? 56!*"

Who? What? Where? In politics, it's not always whether you win or lose or how you play the game, but what kind of numbers you can come up with.

Despite all its built-in weaknesses, Congress sometimes manages to

"AND FOR MY NEXT SURPRISE–"
11/25/70

"IT'S NOT EXACTLY LIKE THE LINCOLN-DOUGLAS DEBATES."
10/13/70

"I WANT TO TELL YOU HOW MUCH I WISH IT WERE POSSIBLE FOR YOU TO WIN THIS RACE."
3/14/69

"NOTHING DOING–WE'RE FIGHTING INFLATION."
5/18/71

come off better than a Chief Executive. As a longtime critic of Congresses (and of Presidential Administrations) let me send up, well, one or two cheers for the recent 91st and 92nd Congresses.

For the record—

It was the White House that widened and deepened our involvement in Indochina, while legislators pushed for speedier withdrawal during the "winding-down" of a war that continued to wind-on-and-on.

It was the legislators who were frustrated by an executive department that obstructed their efforts to obtain information and hid behind an ever-broader interpretation of "executive privilege." This has embraced an ever-expanded White House staff, including more and more policy makers not subject to Senate confirmation and considered by the White House to be beyond questioning by Congress.

The White House has further circumvented Senate authority by negotiating international "executive agreements" that are not called treaties and therefore require no ratification.

It has also refused to spend money at home as legislated by Congress—and disregarded Congressional restrictions on military spending abroad.

When, in addition, an Administraton shows more concern for big campaign contributors than for public welfare measures, Congress—rather than the President—might accurately refer to itself as being conscious of its responsibilities to "all the people." But again—Congress does not get the opportunity to address the nation and punch home that line.

The very means of electing a "President of all the people" was the subject of a reform that originated in Congress. A proposal for amending the Constitution to abolish the electoral college and elect the President by direct popular vote was passed by the House of Representatives in 1969. It very nearly passed the Senate but died there after a filibuster that was almost broken. Presidential support could have made the difference in sending this proposed Amendment to the states. It might even have been ratified in time for the 1972 election—if the White House had wanted it.

The White House was even less enthusiastic about election reform that concerned campaign spending—one of the most vital issues of our time. Costs of campaigns have been so enormous and abuses in campaign financing so great that our political system has been brought to a state of crisis. Money has been dictating who can run for, and frequently who can win, high public office. The amount and importance of "big money" in elections is still great, and obvious to anyone who watched able political aspirants drop by the wayside for lack of funds in the 1970 and 1972 primaries.

In an effort to bring the biggest campaign cost under control, Congress passed a bill in 1970 to regulate television campaigning and campaign spending. The President, who was able to command all the television time he wanted—and who had plenty of big campaign contributors—vetoed this bill.

THE RETURN OF DRACULA
5/13/71

"IT JUST NEEDS A FEW EXTRA INGREDIENTS."

11/10/71

**"LEAVE THIS TO ME, OFFICER—
I'LL DECIDE WHETHER HE HAS A
GOOD EXCUSE."**
11/20/70

The following year, Congress voted for fuller disclosure of funds and for broadening the base of campaign contributions. One of the methods Congress approved to increase public financing of Presidential campaigns was a voluntary one-dollar tax check-off, which a taxpayer could make to any party of his choice (or none at all). But this was part of a general tax bill, which the President threatened to veto if the check-off provision remained in it. When Congress modified this provision to exclude the 1972 campaign, President Nixon signed the bill.

However successful the new law turns out to be, Congress at least made a start in trying to clean up the political environment which has been polluted by the power of "big money" from "big interests."

It also took the lead in efforts to curb environmental pollution. It passed The National Environment Policy Act. It pushed for cleaner air standards, while the White House and the auto industry stood shoulder to shoulder—or bumper to bumper—in trying to hold off effective regulation of automobile exhausts.

Congress also passed a clean-water bill, which the White House (and many big-manufacturer campaign contributors) found impractical or "too expensive." The White House worked to get this bill watered down—or polluted down.

Kin Hubbard wrote, "When a fellow says it hain't the money but the principle o' the thing, it's the money." In Washington it's often the money *and* the principle, depending on who the money is for.

Some of the Administration's greatest efforts were put forth to continue government support for the private-industry supersonic transport, which Congress finally rejected.

The White House also went all-out for a $250-million government guarantee of loans to Lockheed Aircraft, and won by a narrow margin.

However, the same Administration was reluctant to use the money Congress appropriated for school lunch programs—and kept trying to trim it down in ways that would have kept as many as a million and a half children from receiving those lunches.

It was only grudgingly that President Nixon signed the Occupational Safety Act to protect those in hazardous work like mining.

The White House giveth and the White House taketh away, but lately it seems to giveth more to the rich than to the poor.

A Child Development and Day Care bill was vetoed by the President, as were an emergency employment act, a comprehensive manpower training program and public works programs. Add also: appropriations for education and for the Departments of Labor; Health, Education and Welfare; Housing and Urban Development and the Office of Economic Opportunity.

Congressional bills providing for hospital construction and for assistance to hospitals and medical schools to relieve a shortage of doctors fared no better at the White House.

148

"JUST TAKE IT AND GO BACK IN."
7/23/71

"WHAT'S IN A NAME?...A ROSE
BY ANY OTHER NAME..."
2/5/69

"GOT TO TEACH 'EM THE VALUE
OF A DOLLAR."

9/9/71

"WHO SAYS I'M NOT TRYING TO
BRING PEOPLE TOGETHER?"
8/20/71

Many public welfare bills were vetoed outright; and in some cases the Administration simply sat on funds appropriated by Congress.

Congress has also run ahead of the White House in non-money measures, often affecting rights and liberties. It extended the 1965 Voting Rights Act. The House of Representatives, under great pressure from organized groups to pass a so-called "school prayer amendment," mustered enough votes to turn it down. It upheld the courts in maintaining the separation of church and state—but with no word of help from the White House.

Congress *did* originate and pass two other proposed Constitutional Amendments: one to lower the voting age; the other designed to guarantee equal rights for women.

Congress has come quite a way in the field of civil liberties, although it still falls far short of voting to eliminate its more obnoxious investigating committees. But the House of Representatives did something unusual in voting down one committee's request for a contempt citation. The House declined to cite CBS for refusing to produce unused footage for the television program "The Selling of the Pentagon."

For years I have taken whacks at the House Committee on Un-American Activities (which in 1969 legally changed its name to the House Internal Security Committee) and at similar Congressional groups which have sought to determine what is "American" and what associations are proper for "good Americans." In recent years such committees seem to have been less active, or at least less publicity-conscious, though Congress continues appropriating generous funds to them.

Lately it has been the executive department which has seemed more concerned about our associations, our beliefs, and about what organizations are considered proper for us. By 1970, the Subversive Activities Control Board —left with little to do because of federal court decisions striking down McCarthy Era laws—had all but expired. But the White House kept it alive, kept its members on the payroll—and wanted to extend its powers. Congress was reluctant to go along—which was really a reversal of the Executive-Legislative roles of the Fearful Forties and Fifties.

In domestic policies members of Congress have often heard the President belabor them even while following their lead. A good example came in the field of economic legislation.

In August 1970, as the country slid deeper into recession, Congress gave the President economic control powers, which it urged him to use. He scorned their "control" policies, vowing never to use the authority they had given him. But a year later he did use it—with much fanfare about taking bold action by announcing such measures as the wage-price freeze.

Over a period of years, Congressmen have smarted as they have seen Presidents exercise power which the legislators did *not* give—and take actions on which they were not consulted and their advice was not welcome. Presi-

GIANT STEPS

6/22/69

"THAT NEXT APPOINTMENT BETTER BE GOOD."

9/21/71

"DON'T YOU EVEN HAVE A DOG NAMED CHECKERS?"

5/14/69

"NONE OF THE THINGS MY CLIENT DID WERE WRONG, AND HE PROMISES TO STOP DOING THEM."

10/8/69

dent Nixon rubbed salt in that wound after a Congressional declaration that it was the policy of the United States to end "at the soonest practicable date" our military operations in Indochina. Mr. Nixon said that this was without binding force or effect, and "does not reflect my judgment on the way the war should be brought to an end." A simple no-comment-at-all might have been enough.

After doing a slow burn while their powers were being eroded under more than one Administration, it is not too surprising then that many members of Congress found Mr. Nixon's attacks on them a little too much.

Congress probably astonished even itself when in 1971 it voted down a foreign aid bill for the first time since World War II. Some Congressmen were opposed to extensive military aid, some to economic aid provisions. A revised bill was passed later; but Congress had shown some muscle on the combination military-economic "aid" packages.

Congress specifically voted its disapproval of arms to the dictatorships of Greece and Pakistan. But because of "emergency" loopholes, the White House had no trouble continuing such military support. It also didn't hesitate to violate laws passed by Congress forbidding the transfer of military aid from one country to another.

Congress could indeed be tougher. The power of the purse is its ultimate weapon, and probably should be used more often. But many members of Congress are hesitant to cut off funds which would leave them open to accusations of failing to stand behind "our troops" or our "national interests"—as described on television from the White House.

Despite expressions of Congressional disapproval, the war continued. So also did the battles between the White House and Capitol Hill.

The two branches of government at opposite ends of Pennsylvania Avenue come into dramatic conflict in the battle over the third branch of government—the Supreme Court.

Once more the legislative branch found itself at a disadvantage.

When a President decides to make of the Supreme Court a political football, he is playing a game that is hard for his opponents to win. The Senate, by extraordinary effort and teamwork, can hold the line for a while, and can block some plays. But it cannot carry the ball; it can't initiate any plays. It doesn't send up its own nominations, or even "advise."

Since Presidential candidate Nixon had attacked the Supreme Court as it existed in 1968, it was not expected that he would nominate for the highest Court another Hugo Black or an Earl Warren.

What astonished and angered many Senators was the Administration's carelessness in examining the backgrounds of its nominees—and its apparent disregard for the Court as an institution. It not only seemed as if Mr. Nixon didn't know or care about anything but the political views of his nominees; it appeared that he might consciously be trying to make of the nine-man highest court in the land a kind of Little League team.

"ETHICS ARE FOR LIBERALS."
10/3/69

"LADIES AND GENTLEMEN—THE PRESIDENT AND THE VICE PRESIDENT OF THE UNITED STATES."
10/22/69

"NO TIME FOR THOROUGH INVESTIGATIONS—WE'RE IN A HURRY NOW."
1/29/70

Mr. Nixon had earlier expressed admiration for justices like the late Louis Brandeis. But no such regard was evident in any of his appointments to the four vacancies on the Court that came to him as a windfall in his first three years in office.

Judge Warren Burger was confirmed easily for the post of Chief Justice, with the opposition of only three senators. But the nomination of Judge Clement Haynsworth to fill a second vacancy touched off a real fight.

The President, who had earlier made clear that he did not see any reason for replacing a member of a particular religion or region with another of the same, did however want an additional Southerner on the Court. The members of the Senate were not concerned about this. But during the time the Haynsworth nomination was before them, they discovered things that concerned them very much.

As a judge, Haynsworth had voted on cases involving clients of firms in which he held a substantial financial interest; his testimony before the Senate Judiciary Committee conflicted with records of his directorship and other business matters; and in his opinions on civil rights cases he lagged behind the positions previously set by the Supreme Court.

Ironically, he was nominated to replace Justice Abe Fortas—who had resigned from the Court because of criticism of undisclosed financial arrangements. Three months after the Haynsworth nomination was submitted, the judge was turned down by the Senate, 55-45. The fifty-five nay votes included several Republican members of the Senate—among them the Republican leader.

In January 1970, two months after the Haynsworth vote, President Nixon submitted a second candidate for the Court's vacant seat—Judge G. Harrold Carswell, of Florida. This nomination resulted in even more embarrassing disclosures.

It developed that in 1948 Judge Carswell had made a white supremacy speech which was regressive even in the light of much earlier court decisions. In 1956—after Supreme Court desegregation decisions—he helped to convert a Tallahassee public golf course into a private segregated country club. And although he told the Senate he no longer held to the views of his 1948 speech, nothing in his record indicated any earlier conversion or previous support for civil rights.

One of the highlights of the debate, in which Carswell's mediocrity had been cited, was Senator Roman Hruska's defense of the candidate. He asserted that even if Carswell was mediocre, "there are a lot of mediocre judges and people and lawyers, and they are entitled to a little representation, aren't they? We can't have all Brandeises, Frankfurters and Cardozos and stuff like that there."

Carswell's consistent record against equal rights, his mediocrity, and his lack of candor before the Senate committee brought about Senate rejection

"YOU CAN'T HAVE A BALANCED
COURT IF THEY *ALL* BELIEVE IN
CIVIL RIGHTS."

2/13/70

"AH, BUT FOR SEVERAL DAYS NOW
HE'S FOUND THAT SORT OF THING
ABHORRENT."

1/28/70

"HE HAS JUST THE STATURE WE NEED FOR
THE KIND OF BENCH WE WANT."

2/8/70

of a second consecutive nomination to the vacant seat—something unprecedented in Supreme Court nominations. On April 8, 1970, the Carswell nomination was defeated by a vote of 51-45.

The choice of Carswell—and the determination to keep pressing for his
confirmation—has to be one of the most unfortunate episodes in the annals
of Presidential nominations.

In a little over two months, I did some twenty-three cartoons on the
"Carswell case"—partly because I thought the nomination was such an abysmal
example of politics and partly because there was such a widespread feeling
that it was impossible for the Senate to reject two successive nominees.

After the Senate vote I drew the Profiles-In-Courage cartoon to salute
those Senators who, it seemed to me, had put the nation ahead of partisan-
ship, sectionalism, or possible political repercussions.

A day later, President Nixon declared that the Senate vote showed that
"this Senate, as it is presently constituted, will not approve a man from the
South who shares my view of strict construction of the Constitution."

The often used term "strict constructionist" has never been strictly defined, but it obviously was not meant to include men like Justice Hugo Black,
who construed the Bill of Rights to mean exactly what it said. Perhaps the
term referred to Justices who would hold strictly to the President's views.

The President seemed to be—as much as a President can be—in contempt
of the Court and of the Senate, not to mention the rank and file of American
citizens. What must have rankled the Senators particularly was his apparent
notion that their job was simply to ratify his "appointments" to the bench.

The Senate's later confirmation of a Virginia judge to the Supreme Court
showed what hardly needed showing: that Mr. Nixon's earlier characteriza-
tion of the vote against Carswell as "an act of regional discrimination" was
really a Presidential act of Southern-strategy politics in a campaign year.

"I understand the bitter feeling of millions of Americans who live in the
South . . . " said the President after the vote against Carswell. Later in the
year Mr. Carswell ran for the Republican nomination for United States Senator from Florida—a bid in which he received White House support, including speeches by Vice President Agnew. Mr. Carswell, whose Senatorial campaign was consistent with his previous dim record on civil rights, was defeated
by the voters of his own state—and of his (and the President's) own political
party.

During that 1970 campaign President Nixon assailed Congress for not
moving more quickly with its work. Congress does indeed have its hangups.
But it's worth a note that in 1969-70, members of the United States Senate
had to spend an inordinate amount of time defending the integrity of the
United States Supreme Court. The naming of worthier nominees by a Chief
Executive could have saved the Senators many workdays.

The Senate subsequently confirmed the nominations of Justice Harry A.

"DON'T BE PICKY—THERE'S
NOTHING WRONG WITH HIM
EXCEPT HIS RECORD."

2/24/70

"SO IT CAN'T PASS INSPECTION, IT'S
HOT, AND IT'S GOT PHONY PAPERS
—I BEEN TOLD TO UNLOAD IT."

3/18/70

1970 CHAPTER

4/9/70

"IMAGINE THE KIND OF RADICAL-
LIBERALS WHO TURNED DOWN THIS
SPLENDID FELLOW!"

9/24/70

Blackmun (unanimously); Justice Lewis F. Powell (with one dissenting vote); and Justice William H. Rehnquist (68–26). The reluctance of the Senate leadership to delay a vote on Rehnquist, despite a record that showed more legal cleverness than concern for Constitutional rights and liberties, may very well have indicated that it was just plain tired of fighting over Court nominees.

The four justices who were confirmed may have given the President a "Nixon Court" even if not composed of the members he would have liked best.

Still, the Senate battles over the Court were worthwhile. And the decisions to make a stand for the third branch of government may have inspired the legislative branch to stand up for itself as well.

Congress pressed somewhat harder—though not hard enough—for its proper role in decisions on war and foreign policy. It pressed for more public information. It resisted some pressures for government guarantees to big businesses. Not so long ago, a supersonic transport would have whizzed through Congress with a deafening sonic boom.

Congress also served notice that a "foreign aid" label, like a "stand-by-the-Chief" label, was no longer good enough to insure passage of executive "package" bills—even though Congress couldn't actually mobilize itself to check Presidential power.

And so, in my own little message to Congress, I'd like to say: You fellows have been doing a lot better than the White House would have us believe—sometimes standing up where it counts. But you need to do more.

There are many cases where just a little tougher stance or a few more votes would do it.

For example, instead of just balking at supporting a Subversive Activities Control Board, you could knock it out—and save us nearly half a million dollars besides.

You originated a tax revision bill, which even made a dent in the oil-depletion allowance—but you can do a lot more tax reforming, even though the White House doesn't seem enthusiastic about that.

Your attempt to limit individual farm subsidy payments was a good effort, even if big-business "farmers" have been able to get around it. You might have another go at that too.

You can also do more reforming of political campaign laws.

You've finally been taking a closer look at our enormous, expensive arms programs, and goodness knows they need it.

You've been trying to pry more information out of the executive branch; and you're going to have to work still harder at that.

You fellows are going to have to find ways to turn back arbitrary extensions of executive power and privilege. This means getting yourselves organized—or reorganized—to act as a more effective branch of government.

You need to stand up to the White House—and do more about putting your own Houses in order.

"THIS HERE BOY IS A STRICT
CONSTRUCTIONIST. HE'LL UPHOLD
THE STRAIGHT OLD U.S.
CONSTITUTION WITHOUT ALL
THOSE FANDANGLED AMENDMENTS
ABOUT PEOPLE'S RIGHTS."
11/16/71

"AND NOW—FROM THE SAME
PEOPLE WHO GAVE YOU
G. HARROLD CARSWELL—"
11/24/71

"ONE SMALL STEP FOR TAXPAYERS
—ONE GIANT LEAP FOR
POLITICIANS"

8/8/69

FOR THE CHAMPIONSHIP OF
THE UNITED STATES
11/17/71

Well, anyhow—the President has said that "there is a tendency of some in the media . . . to emphasize a negative." So I've talked about some of the positive things you've done—things he somehow doesn't get around to mentioning in a positive way himself.

Cheers for those things. But you still have a way to go. Which reminds me—that seniority system has to go!

And about that so-called *Congressional Record* you fellows put out!——

HAUNTED HOUSE

7/12/70

HIGH PUBLIC OFFICE

1/12/72

Campaign Flight

THIS IS going to be a quick hop over recent national campaigns—or parts of them.

In looking back, a few things stand out.

One is the crazyquilt presidential primary system which may or may not coincide with the polls—or influence the polls—or decide a nomination.

In recent years the competition for the presidential nomination has been greater among Democrats than among Republicans. In 1968, Democrats were running for President in primaries even before the withdrawal of Democratic leader Lyndon Johnson, the incumbent President. With the election obviously up for grabs, it might have been expected that in the Republican presidential primaries, competition would be even fiercer.

There wasn't any.

Despite the fact that Richard M. Nixon in his last two races for public office had been a loser, he had no real opposition in the 1968 presidential primaries.

To a large extent, recent campaigns and elections seem to have been influenced by people who were not there—beginning with voters who didn't appear at the polling places.

Mr. Nixon has generally had his best luck in elections when he was not there on the campaign trail. In 1970, when he campaigned with the full power of the Presidency, his party had a bad year. In 1971 and 1972, he probably did his most effective campaigning when he was not in the U.S., but traveling abroad in what some called "the Moscow and Peking primaries."

The White House press conference most helpful to Mr. Nixon politically took place when he was not there. It occurred in 1966 when President Johnson met with the press immediately upon returning from a trip to Asia. Mr. Johnson, who seemed to be suffering from jet-lag, went into a rambling attack on Mr. Nixon—who at the time did not seem to be the best prospect for 1968. Shortly afterward, Mr. Nixon was replying on nationwide television—and was off and running.

Among those who were not there in 1968 were Republicans like Nelson Rockefeller, who did not even enter their party's primaries; police and demonstrators not inside the Democratic convention hall but outside in the streets and parks of Chicago; and Senator Eugene McCarthy, who had been there in a very useful and important way opposing President Johnson's Vietnam policies in primaries as early as New Hampshire—but who was not there when his support might have made the difference in the fall election campaign.

Senator McCarthy still said, as late as October 1971, that in the 1968 elec-

"HE REALLY SHRINKS ON YOU,
DOESN'T HE?"

11/12/68

"I THINK YOU'LL FIND THAT
CAMERA GIVING A DISTORTED
PICTURE OF EVENTS."

9/10/68

"FIRST OF ALL, CAN SHE SUPPORT
ME IN THE MANNER TO WHICH I
HAVE BECOME ACCUSTOMED?"

11/14/68

AMERICAN POLITICAL PROCESS:
'63 . . . '68 . . . '72 . . .

5/16/72

tion the differences between the Republican and Democratic presidential candidates were so small they made no difference at all. But by May 1972, after the bombing and mining of North Vietnamese ports began, he was calling for President Nixon's impeachment.

Although President Johnson's surprising announcement of March 1968 took him out of the presidential race—and though he was not there at the Democratic convention either—it was nevertheless "Johnson's War" that loomed over the 1968 election.

During the closing days of that campaign, President Johnson was working to get the Paris peace negotiations off dead center. But once more the political campaign was influenced by a man who took no direct part in it—General Nguyen Van Thieu. By dragging his feet on the negotiations, General Thieu played a role in our presidential election—and he was apparently pleased by the result.

Also not present, but very much in people's thoughts, were all the American soldiers still in Vietnam—and all who had died there.

Three of our most prominent Americans were gone too: President John F. Kennedy, The Reverend Dr. Martin Luther King, Jr., and Senator Robert F. Kennedy. Had it not been for these three deaths—and the violence (followed by the backlash) that came after the King assassination—our elections and our history since 1963 would have been quite different.

We think of countries ruled by rotating military leaders as being influenced by death and violence. But there is probably no country in which these factors have so strongly affected national leadership as in the U.S. during the last decade.

The assassination attempt on Governor George Wallace marked the third presidential election since 1960 in which gunshots figured significantly.

Money and murder—campaign contributions and guns—stand out among the biggest factors in recent national elections.

Some effort is being made by Congress to bring campaign spending under control. We can at least make the same effort with guns. We can try to prevent that kind of "bullet voting."

Effective control of these weapons might well save some of our political leaders from being gunned down. Certainly they'd save a lot of voters who would still be alive and well to take part in elections.　■

"DEAR, DID HE SAY WHICH CANDIDATES ARE *FOR* BOMBING, BURNING, RIOTING AND MUGGING?"
10/27/70

"SPIRO AND I HAVE BEEN DOING EVERYTHING WE COULD FOR CAMPUS UNREST."
12/15/70

"NEVER MIND WHY—JUST GET RID OF ALL THOSE STUPID BALLOON PICTURES."
1/21/70

"HAVE YOU NO SENSE OF PRIORITIES!"
10/16/70

"WHAT DO YOU MEAN,
'RECESSION'?"

10/25/70

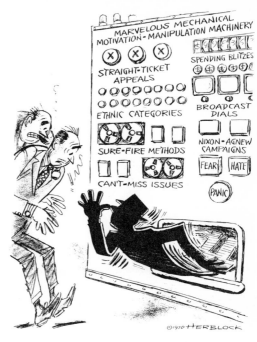

VOTER PROFILE

11/5/70

"CALL THE NASA SPACE CENTER—
I'VE GOT AN IDEA FOR ANOTHER
TRIP BEFORE NOVEMBER 1972."

10/13/71

12/1/71

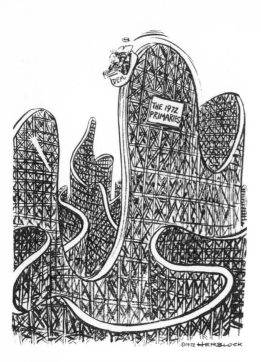

"WHEEE – GOOD GRIEF! – WHEEE
– OH, MY GOSH! – "

5/14/72

4/28/72

"GOODNESS, COULD THERE BE
ANYONE LIKE THAT?"

4/28/71

"A FUNNY THING HAPPENED ON
THE WAY BACK FROM THE
BARBECUE. I RAN INTO SOME DAMN
DEMOCRATS IN A PRIMARY – "

5/12/72

CAMPAIGN BUS

8/13/71

TIP OF THE ICEBERG

6/13/72

**"FUNNY, YOU DON'T *LOOK*
DEMOCRATIC."**

5/18/72

**"PLEASE! A WORLD FIGURE LIKE
THE PRESIDENT CAN NOT BE
BOTHERED WITH THESE DOMESTIC
DETAILS."**

6/22/72

"JUST AS I SUSPECTED ALL ALONG—
THAT GENTLE GEORGE McGOVERN
WAS A STALKING HORSE FOR
MIGHTY GEORGE McGOVERN."

6/8/72

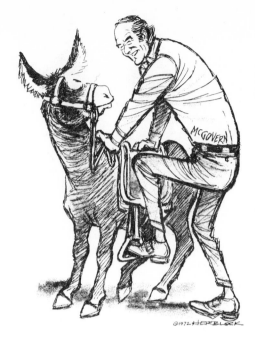

"EASY, NOW—STEADY—HERE WE
GO—"

6/9/72

"WHEW!"

7/12/72

"AND WHEN YOU FELLOWS HOLD
YOUR CONVENTION HERE IN
AUGUST, WE HOPE YOU'LL HAVE A
GOOD TIME TOO."

7/14/72

"EXACTLY—WE'LL SIT OUT THE REST
OF THIS CENTURY."

7/20/72

"AND THERE'S FACILITIES FOR
NATIONAL TV AND PRESS
SERVICES AS WELL AS
INTERNATIONAL TELEPHONE AND
TELEGRAPH—DID I SAY SOMETHING
WRONG?"

5/5/72

"AREN'T YOU SURPRISED AND
THRILLED?"

7/25/72

"DON'T BE CHICKEN—TRY IT JUST
ONCE MORE."

1/29/69

"I'D FEEL BETTER WITHOUT THAT
GUY SITTING IN THE BACK OF THE
COCKPIT."

9/15/70

"OUT, DAMNED 'SPOTS'!"

10/6/70

"RELAX—THIS'LL BLOW OVER TOO."

5/17/72

"DEARIE, IN THIS STORY YOU'VE GOT TO FIND THE PRINCE CHARMING FIRST."

/25/72

"MAN, WE WERE LUCKY—WE RODE ON THOSE THINGS BEFORE ANYONE REALIZED HOW TERRIBLE THEY ARE."

6/27/72

THE WINNER

11/24/70

"WHAT AM I DOING HERE?"

12/21/69

Foreign Policy Made Easy

INTERNATIONAL RELATIONS have always been complex and confusing except to those who think we should tell the rest of the world to go away. We have our Kremlinologists; the Russians undoubtedly have their White-Houseologists. And after watching the United States for a few decades, Asia is probably full of people who regard us as inscrutable.

The generation of Americans that grew up right after World War II had a particularly hard time sorting things out because nations they first heard of as enemies became our friends; and some gallant wartime allies became cold-war enemies.

Many of those who grew up *before* World War II had other problems. Some discovered that in pre-Pearl Harbor days they had been "prematurely anti-fascist." And if they had also been early critics of Stalinism they might have been "prematurely anti-communist" as well.

In the postwar period of "emerging nations" it turned out that some of our great traditional allies were "imperialists" and "colonialists."

Later on, we also discovered that what emerged in *some* of those brand new nations was some of the same old brand of authoritarianism and aggression.

Since 1968, much has been done to simplify our international relations and to resolve the vexing problems posed by dealing with "communists" and "fascists." We now have Foreign Policy Made Easy.

On the basis of completely impeachable sources and papers not only secret but completely non-existent, it is now possible to disclose how this came about. The policy was established after a quick exhaustive study of the world which took place in the White House basement early in 1969. This top-secret night session was interrupted only by urgent telephone calls to Dr. Henry Kissinger, who in each case replied cryptically, "I told you not to call me at the office."

This conference engaged the highest officials of the Administration, including the Joint Chiefs of Staff and the White House political advisers. At its conclusion, the result was relayed to Secretary of State William Rogers, who promptly called a news conference to tell reporters that he felt fine.

Briefly, the members of the top-level White House strategy meeting decided to divide the nations of the world into two broad categories: democracies and dictatorships. Following this basic decision, it was relatively easy to adopt the policy: We would be nicer to the dictatorships.

"NOW, ARE THERE ANY DEMOCRACIES WE HAVEN'T OFFENDED OR ANY DICTATORSHIPS WE HAVEN'T COZIED UP TO?"

12/10/71

PREVIOUSLY UNFORTIFIED BORDER

10/12/71

"AND NOW, TO DROWN OUT ANY COMPLAINTS—"

10/29/71

"THERE'S SOMETHING ABOUT A SOLDIER—"

11/23/69

It was this policy which enabled a President—who had spent his entire career belaboring opponents who tried to establish better relations with countries like China and Russia—to plan friendly trips to China and Russia.

It also allowed him to do this without missing a beat in continued close cooperation with the Franco government in Spain, and increased public support for the ruling junta which had put an end to democracy in Greece.

What all these governments had in common, and what made everything completely consistent, was that they were dictatorships. There was now no need to distinguish between great nations like Russia and China (which had no democratic traditions and whose governments existed despite our opposition) and governments like that of the Greek colonels, who were propped up by us.

The be-nicer-to-dictatorships policy was what Robert L. Asher would describe in his writings about colonialism as a simple rule of under-the-thumb.

The corollary of the be-nicer-to-dictatorships policy was be-tougher-to-democracies. We no longer needed to have any hesitancy about giving the back of our hand to nations like Japan, Canada and India, for example. As one Administration official said laughingly when asked about the Japanese and Canadian dismay over the imposition of a 10 percent import tax, "We really shook 'em up, didn't we?"

Indeed we did. Both Japan and Canada also worried that they might be shaken up in another way by the biggest-ever underground nuclear explosion which we announced would take place at Amchitka, Alaska. Our nuclear blast did not create any immediate damage such as great destructive tidal waves. There were only the waves of ill-will generated by our cavalier attitude toward governments which had regarded themselves as our friends.

The new international policy was not arrived at frivolously. Prudence dictates that government relationships long established should not be changed for light and transient causes. The dictatorship-democracy policy not only makes foreign affairs more simple and tidy; it *promotes* simplicity and tidiness.

Democracies do not put a premium on order. They go in for free speech, which creates a dissonance. This is very distracting and disturbing. And with democratic institutions like free assembly, free press and free elections, such governments are likely to be changeable. Who knows when opinions might shift and a group in power be dismissed?

Dictatorships, on the other hand, are more stable. True, there are occasional changes in personnel, but such changes are generally made by a good solid ruling group. In the short run, at least, dictatorships can be depended on to keep on dictating—and to make plans without regard to

"AND I'M STAYING RIGHT HERE TO
GUARD IT FOR YOU."
9/24/68

"IT GIVES YOU A CHANCE TO BE
RIGHT ON THE SPOT WHEN
TROUBLE BREAKS OUT."
1/6/70

"WE NEED HIM TO HELP FIGHT
THE COMMUNIST REVOLT — AS SOON
AS HE GETS IT STARTED."
6/4/69

"EVERYBODY OUT! EVERYBODY
DANCE IN THE STREETS! LET'S GO!"
4/15/69

voters, congresses, parliaments and other flibbertigibbet things associated with free countries. They are no-nonsense outfits that you can do business with. And they arrange things tidily.

Take the Greek colonels, for instance. When members of the press print things the government doesn't approve of, it takes care of them with dispatch—and none of those expensive long-drawn-out trials that cost us so much money and get so much news space in our country. That's real national order. The Greek rulers also have arrested judges who believed in an independent judiciary. We don't have that kind of speedy justice over here, or that kind of tidy solution to the problems of government executives.

Let the word go forth to friend and foe alike that Neatness Counts.

Many American tourists have returned from Greece to assure us they heard no complaints about the dictatorship. What better proof that all is well there—in a happy land not plagued by demonstrations or dissension. True, there are Greek citizens who cannot leave the country—and spokesmen for Greek democracy who would find it dangerous to return home. But this is all part of an orderly plan. So are the prisons and torture chambers, although these are not included in the tourists' itineraries. But those who are interested in such things are generally the kind of Americans who tend to dwell on the bad news and who don't talk about what's *right* with the Greek colonels.

Along with the tourists and increased American arms aid, there have also been official American visitors.

Secretary of Commerce Maurice Stans, in April 1971, praised the "sense of security" the Greek government gave American companies operating there. He also brought regards from President Nixon for "the way in which the two countries are working together" and best wishes "for the continued welfare and prosperity of the people of Greece." Secretary Stans said the United States was proud to be one of Greece's largest trading partners and her principal source of foreign exchange. He added that "given the continued economic stability and the continuing political stability, there is no limit to the growth that can take place in Greece."

There also seemed to be no limit to the enthusiasm of our government for that kind of "political stability." Mr. Stans regarded the presence of "nine ministers and deputy ministers of the Government of Greece" who attended his talk as a "a compliment to the Government of the United States."

To the Nixon Administration since 1969, it was apparently a proud moment when a representative of the little old Government of the United States got that kind of attention from really *professional* Law-and-Order people like the Greek colonels. That kind of touching compliment makes all the support for a dictatorship worth while.

An even more impressive reception was given to Vice President Spiro

"I RECOGNIZE AND APPRECIATE THE ACHIEVEMENTS THAT ARE GOING FORWARD UNDER THE PRESENT GREEK GOVERNMENT."
—SPIRO T. AGNEW

10/21/71

"I DON'T OFTEN SHARE MY TREASURE WITH FOREIGNERS."
4/8/69

"YOU MEAN YOU MIGHT NOT LET ME STAY ON FOR ANOTHER FIVE-YEAR FUN-FILLED CRUISE?"
6/3/69

"WE HAVE TO PAY HIM PROTECTION MONEY—IT ENTITLES US TO PROTECT HIM."
3/18/69

T. Agnew when *he* went to Greece a few months later. He was personally met at the airport by Premier George Papadopoulos, the dictator himself, who accompanied him on a ride through the streets of Athens. Mr. Agnew said, "I recognize and appreciate the achievements that are going forward under the present Greek government."

Mr. Agnew was presented with Greece's highest medal. It hardly seemed too much.

Our government later worked out plans to supply the rulers of Greece with an aerospace plant and Phantom jets. Such things give both governments a "sense of security." And it gives our arms contractors a warm and comfortable feeling too.

Eventually there may be a revolution in Greece, and people whose hopes have been dashed by the world's greatest democracy may end up embracing communism. In that case we can send more arms to the Greek dictators—and then maybe American advisers—and then troops—and then B-52 bombers. . . .

We have long maintained bases in Spain, which, ever since the Franco dictatorship took over, has also been billed as a bulwark against communism. You might think a government like that would be glad to have a cold-war ally like us maintain armed power in its country for possible use against a great common enemy. But we have had to pay through the nose for the privilege of retaining our bases there, with General Franco constantly escalating the price and adding new diplomatic demands as the old cold-war bases became more obsolete. He might be called a very dear friend of the U.S. So dear that from the standpoint of American taxpayers the reign in Spain has mostly been a pain.

In the days before the intercontinental ballistic missile and the nuclear submarine, our arrangements with Spain were considered by many in Washington as an unpleasant necessity. But with the be-nicer-to-dictators policy, we became worried about any possible slight to the Franco government. On February 19, 1969—a month after inauguration day—a "sensitivity briefing guide" was issued for American personnel in Spain. It included such evidences of sensitivity as these:

> Do not discuss Hitler or Nazi Germany. Since Hitler and Mussolini provided military aid to General Franco during the civil war, [Franco] is against derogatory references [about them]. As you may never have a favorable reference, it approaches a universal prohibition.
>
> Anticommunism in general is good and usable. Favorable references to communism and pro or con discussions of communism should be avoided.
>
> Dictatorship and references to it should be avoided. Be especially wary of comparisons between dictatorships and freedom. . . .
>
> Do not talk about religion in Spain. . . . However, if someone has visited a church recently and wants to describe the visit, this is permitted. Talking about Spanish restrictions on Protestant religious activities is *not* permitted.

"WE EAGLES HAVE TO STICK
TOGETHER."

6/25/69

"BROTHER, THE LAW-AND-ORDER
PROBLEM IS GETTING FIERCE."
12/22/70

"HOW AWFUL! IT'S A GOOD THING I TOOK
OFF MY DARK GLASSES IN TIME TO SEE
THIS."

12/8/71

Without such instructions, people brought up with crude American ideas about freedom might not know how to behave in dealing with a sensitive regime like Franco's, which was at the time reverting to some of the worst repressions of its long reign.

If our government felt bases in Spain were all that important, you might suppose they were our sole outpost in that entire area of the world. But right next door to Spain is Portugal—and somewhat west, the Azores, which Portugal controls.

For many years we've also used air bases in the Azores. In 1971 we concluded a formal agreement for continued use of the bases—and for providing credits, aid and increasing trade with Portugal.

If there is one government in Europe more widely and thoroughly disliked than Franco's, it is that of Portugal—the last colonial power in Africa and one widely identified with racism.

Nearly two hundred years after the Declaration of Independence, we were leaving no rock unturned in looking for dictatorships and colonialists to be nice to. And to make absolutely sure that everyone understood the New American Revolution abroad, our arrangements with such governments had to be sealed with full public ceremonies.

With Vice President Agnew in Spain for "National Day" festivities in 1971, our government helped Franco celebrate the thirty-fifth anniversary of his military uprising against the Spanish Republic. And later that year, President Nixon gave a high-profile demonstration of our new, improved ties with Spain's colonial neighbor by traveling to Portugal and meeting the Prime Minister of that country personally.

The be-nicer-to-dictators policy probably met its greatest test in Pakistan, where our government leaders managed to achieve a diplomatic debacle only by showing nerves of iron—with brains to match.

Pakistan's first election in twenty-three years was held in 1970 and resulted in a victory for the party supported by the populous East Pakistanis. Military ruler Yahya Kahn, who governed from West Pakistan, promptly abrogated the results of the election. A few months later he initiated what might be called the "permanent solution of the majority problem" by sending troops into East Pakistan. There, over a period of months, they slaughtered hundreds of thousands of the inhabitants. Millions more fled to India, where the influx of refugees created a serious problem for that country.

But in that crisis of the new policy we stood firm in showing that we were not bleeding-heart liberals concerned about freedom, human lives, a decent respect to the opinions of mankind or other silly idealistic notions that work.

Through eight months of terror in East Pakistan, the government in Washington continued sending military aid to dictator Yahya Khan, accompanied by no word of reproach.

"ANY MORE IDEAS?"

12/22/71

"PLAY IT AGAIN, GAMAL."

10/7/69

"THEY'RE WILLING TO FORGET THE
PAST—ALL THEY ASK IS THAT YOU
FORGET IT TOO."

7/26/70

But when the terrorized Bengalis fought back, aided and then joined by India in fighting Pakistan, our government expressed outrage—against India, of course.

India and the Bengalis won that war and established the independent state of Bangladesh. This left our government in a somewhat embarrassing position—especially after the leak of a top-level meeting where Dr. Kissinger said he was getting hell from the President every half-hour "that we are not being tough enough against India." The President wanted to "tilt in favor of Pakistan."

Anyone who has ever played a pinball machine must know how the President felt when that word TILT flashed across the country—and when the war actually tilted in favor of democratic India instead of the military dictatorship we supported. We had tilted so far toward the Pakistani military rulers that we fell flat on our faces. But who'd have thought that a government as corrupt and ruthless as that of Yahya Khan would be toppled? Well, you can't win 'em all.

In the Middle East we also adopted something of a tilt. In this case, our tougher attitude toward a democracy caused us to tilt so far backward that for a time we could not see what was going on. We didn't call it a tilt—we called it a balance. This was a neat policy of reducing international arms supplies to the Middle East area by "balancing" Russia's all-out aid to Egypt with our holding back the sale of modern American planes to Israel.

Incidentally, one of the strange and suspicious things about those Israelis was that they wanted to *buy* arms and to *pay* for them. They also defended themselves without our having to promote "Israelization." Dictatorships don't do unsettling things like that. They take our support for free, or take our arms at knock-down prices—and, as in the case of Spain, they sometimes stick us with a stiff overcharge besides. Had Israel been a military dictatorship it might have had all the arms it wanted for free, and probably American installations, troops and advisers to boot—or to boot around. Our Administration planners obviously felt that a government which is supported by its people, pays for its own defense and fights its own battles just can't be kosher.

Besides, a country like that takes all the fun out of *giving*.

The Israelis had other quaint and disturbing notions. They did not think they were protected by more "assurances" of the kind that had left them to look after their own precarious survival on previous occasions. In addition to this, they had the radical idea that the way for countries which have been at war to make peace was to negotiate peaceful settlements.

This was one of the ideas that seemed wildly impractical to an American government which had always done its own peace negotiating.

**"GOSH, WE'VE BEEN SO BUSY
TAKING BOWS, WE COULDN'T WATCH
EVERYTHING."**

8/18/70

**"GOODNESS, WE'RE NOT TRYING TO
LEAN ON YOU—WE WANT YOU TO
WORK OUT YOUR OWN WAY OF
ACCEPTING OUR TERMS."**

3/28/71

**"VERRRRY INTERRRRESTING—BUT
SHTUPID."**

5/7/70

**"I FOLLOW A STRICTLY HANDS-OFF
POLICY."**

8/26/71

The U.S. did help achieve a cease-fire in the cross-canal warfare which had been initiated against Israeli forces by Egypt in 1969. But the Administration, with visions of Peace Prizes dancing in its head, then proceeded to put the heat on the Israelis to accept whatever settlement the U.S. (and the Russians and the Arabs) decided to press upon them. This consisted of having Israel give up all—or almost all—of the territory it hung on to after turning back the Nasser threat of annihilation in 1967.

So intent was the U.S. on forcing Israel to accept a settlement that it not only kept that democracy from obtaining new arms, but initially overlooked the increasing Russian presence in Egypt. Our government did not seem impressed by Russian advisers, Russian planes and Russian pilots— even when they crossed the Suez to tangle with Israeli planes. The U.S. was officially oblivious also to new Russian missile sites installed close to the Suez canal in violation of the cease-fire agreement.

It was not, in fact, till the Israeli government produced unmistakable proof of the new missile installations that the U.S. Government reluctantly conceded their existence.

Eventually the Administration stopped pressuring Israel to accept an unsatisfactory settlement, allowed it to resume purchases of arms, and returned to friendlier relations with it. This improved condition was brought about by Israeli firmness (previously called intransigence). It was perhaps only coincidental that the added touch of common sense in Washington became evident with the approach of the 1972 U.S. election. Despite a barrage of propaganda designed to erase the memory of events preceding the Six-Day War, Americans were not quite ready to think of Israel as an aggressive nation which had simply decided to march forth and conquer some territory.

There were no such sticky problems in dealing with the government of President Thieu in Vietnam, who asked only for continued American support, and who said frankly that he wanted to see President Nixon re-elected. The be-nicer-to-dictators policy made it possible for our government to view with equanimity, if not a public display of joy, the one-man "election" which kept that general in power.

Mr. Nixon said, "We would have preferred . . . a contested election somewhat along the lines that would meet our standard." But, as in the case of Greece, a little lip service seemed good enough for democratic hopes, while military government somehow seemed to meet "our standard" quite well. Our standard for Thailand and Cambodia didn't seem to take in self-government at all.

In Latin America, American policy of other days called for a mere handshake for dictatorships but an embrace for democracies.

In 1960, John F. Kennedy had said, "We must end our open and warm backing of dictators. Our honors must be reserved for democratic leaders, not despots."

"I CHRISTEN THEE 'ACTION FOR PROGRESS.'"

11/2/69

"DON'T TAKE IT PERSONALLY—IT'S A GENERAL POLICY ON ALMOST EVERYTHING."

10/9/69

"BUT SOME ... ARE MORE EQUAL THAN OTHERS."

2/16/69

"WHEN KISSINGER GETS HERE, MAYBE WE CAN FIND OUT WHAT'S GOING ON IN WASHINGTON."

10/7/71

There was some erosion of this policy under President Johnson, who acted with unseemly haste in sending greetings to the leaders of the Brazilian military coup in 1964. But since 1968 our "standard" has warmly embraced Latin dictatorships and offered little more than handshakes for democracies.

In 1971, for the first time in ten years, a Latin American dictator was feted at the White House in a state visit. President Nixon and Brazilian military ruler General Emilio Médici stood on the White House balcony within sight of Brazilians and other democratic sympathizers who held a banner reading: *Stop Complicity In Brazilian Tortures.* Shortly after, Mr. Nixon and the dictator went in to dinner. The President of the United States toasted the general and said, "We know that as Brazil goes, so will go the rest of that Latin American continent."

Latin Americans who still lived under democratic governments or in hope of freedom might well have felt that what Mr. Nixon was doing was, as Governor George Wallace might put it, to "send them a message."

White House adviser Robert Finch later traveled to some of our Latin neighbors on a trip that seemed more designed to sell American arms than historic American ideals. In South America he visited four countries—all dictatorships.

The U.S.-Latin American Alliance for Progress, initiated in 1961 to promote political and economic democracy, never reached its potential. But what has now come to the forefront has been a kind of domestic Alliance for Profit. The U.S. Administration, which had announced that the Greek dictatorship gave American companies a "sense of security," made clear to our southern neighbors that the U.S. Government stood right behind U.S. corporations in those countries.

Indeed, our current government has not only stood behind big American corporate interests, but has tagged along behind them.

Our official leaders have complained about advantages which they said countries like Japan and Germany enjoyed over us. But at the same time they were working to improve economic relations with countries like China and Russia—which, they had been telling us all these years, were slave-labor countries. Those Americans who had worried about the consequences of buying a godless, atheistic Polish ham could now see their most business-oriented political leaders eager to promote trade with disciples of Marx and Lenin.

With a recession at home, it might be that trade followed the flagging economy.

Anyhow, it turned out that in the eyes of large corporations and a political Administration representing them, ideology was not so important after all. Business is business, and big business is bigger-and-bigger business.

Some of those big business corporations are bigger than many of the

GREAT LEAP FORWARD

4/8/71

7/18/71

nations we deal with. The International Telephone and Telegraph Company, for example, tried to interest the U.S. Government in acting to prevent the democratically elected President of Chile from taking office. But ITT was less successful in influencing U.S. policy in Chile than at home.

Of course, meetings between our government officials and the big corporate U.S. powers like ITT are not as widely publicized as meetings with big-power leaders abroad. It is at those international summit meetings with government leaders that press and television coverage is welcome.

Indeed, it was through the magic of television that an Asian power denounced by our leaders as aiding North Vietnam in killing Americans suddenly became a friendly host. This greatest of television events in foreign policy was the 1972 Presidential visit to Commu—oops—the People's Republic of China.

It was not many years before that Secretary of State John Foster Dulles, enthusiastically supported by Vice President Richard M. Nixon, forbade even the travel of American newsmen to the People's Repub—oops—Communist China. Now, here were planeloads of American newsmen—particularly television commentators and crews who could bring the entire week's Presidential visit live by satellite—right there in China with him. Well, newsmen and TV commentators are all right, it seems, when they're covering the right news and not commenting unfavorably on U.S. political leaders.

The first announcement of the China trip was astonishing to many people but not to Senator Warren Magnuson of Washington, Chairman of the Senate Commerce Committee. In the days of the Eisenhower-Nixon Administration, Senator Magnuson wanted to make a fact-finding trip to China with a view to promoting trade there. He hit the ceiling when he discovered in 1960 that Vice President Nixon was trying to promote for himself a trip to China to meet Mao Tse-tung. As reported by the late George Dixon in a 1960 column, "the Vice President thinks that a trip to Red China within the next few months would boost his stock back to where it was after his historic quarrel with Nikita Khrushchev in a Red Russian kitchen . . . and his 'image' will be so gigantic he'll overshadow any stay-at-home Democratic opponent."

Senator Magnuson guaranteed to raise hell if he and a Senate colleague were barred from making their non-political trip to China and the Vice President was allowed to make his political trip. None of them went to China—in *that* Presidential election year.

Twelve years later, with China close to admission to the United Nations, and after signals from Peking that it wanted contact, the trip was announced and took place as millions watched.

It was certainly high time we did some public fence-mending with China—though, of course, our government *had* been engaging in talks with

THE YEAR THE YANKEES LOST THE PENNANT

10/27/71

THE TWO-NIXON CHINA POLICY

10/31/71

"ROLL THOSE U.N. SHOTS AGAIN, AND LET'S GET THE NAMES OF THE GUYS THAT ARE SMILING."

10/28/71

"GOOD GRIEF, YOUR EXCELLENCY! THE SCHEDULE SAYS *WE'RE* SUPPOSED TO BE VISITING *THEM* TODAY."

10/26/71

representatives of Mao China in Warsaw for many years. It's only fair to give credit where credit is due. President Nixon did what no Democratic President could have done without being attacked by Republican party leader Richard M. Nixon.

It might also be said that, while Presidents Kennedy and Johnson negotiated with Russia on nuclear controls, only President Nixon could have conceded Russia nuclear parity without being condemned by Mr. Nixon.

President Johnson called off his 1968 Moscow summit meeting after the Russian invasion of Czechoslovakia. But I wish Mr. Nixon had seized the opportunity Mr. Johnson provided for negotiating an arms agreement with Russia in 1969—instead of waiting till 1972.

I also wish that Mr. Nixon had shown a greater desire for better relations with a democracy like India.

After we had antagonized India by our chilly treatment of Premier Indira Gandhi and by our "tilt" against that country in the war for Bangladesh independence, an Administration spokesman explained that "we didn't 'lose India' because we never had India in the first place." Ah, if only the leader of this Administration had thought of that in all those years when he was denouncing the Democrats for having "lost China"—after all the aid they had given the government of Chiang Kai-shek. Had he only come up with a phrase like that earlier, he might never have had to rediscover China.

Curiously enough, the Chinese summit fitted in with the general pattern of our relationships to dictatorships and democracies—even aside from the fact that a "two-China policy" enabled us to support two non-democratic rulers at once.

Of real importance was the fact that the Presidential China trip was announced without any notice to Japan. This democratic government and faithful ally in Asia found itself ignored in the plans for the visit of an American President to the other great Asian power. Whether the U.S. Administration was intentionally snubbing Japan or whether it felt the political value of the surprise announcement at home outweighed the effect on our Asian ally, U.S.-Japanese relations were damaged.

While the President was preparing for his visit to mainland China, the U.S. voted *against* the admission of that China to the United Nations. More than that, the White House publicly expressed the President's anger at the "glee" he thought some U.N. delegates showed in voting to admit mainland China and expel Taiwan China.

So what we were officially mad at was the voting in the U.N. Assembly—which, for all its faults, was more democratic than the governments of "Mao China" or "Chiang China." It was never made clear just what we expected the United Nations to do while arrangements for the Presidential visit to China were going forward—or whether our leaders felt it would have pleased them more if the delegates of other U.N. countries had scowled or turned away from the cameras while they were voting.

**"IT LOOKS LIKE MORE
NON-MUSHROOM WEATHER TO ME."**
5/30/72

5/31/72

"DR. KISSINGER, I PRESUME?"

6/16/72

Well, the U.N. Assembly was another one of those voting bodies, and our President was officially angry with it too.

As for the future of Taiwan, we left this to be straightened out between the governments of Mao Tse-tung and Chiang Kai-shek—or their successors. Perhaps that's the neatest way for leaders to settle things.

Still, after all our talk about self-determination in the southern part of Vietnam, it would have been nice to have heard something said about the *people* of Taiwan. They might like a chance to have a say about their future. But if they could do that, then the next thing you know they might want to have free elections—and free assembly—and a free press——

When you don't deal with leaders who have things firmly in hand—or under the thumb—you're always likely to run into troublemakers like that.

**"DID YOU SAY THE MAGIC WORDS,
'LAW AND ORDER'?"**
4/15/70

194

ENDANGERED AMERICAN SPECIES

8/11/71

The Law-and-Order Gang

"LAWS OF UNIVERSE PUT INTO QUESTION" read a headline in *The New York Times* early in 1972. Astronomical observations revealed objects that seemed "to be moving faster than light, contrary to assumed physical law." This left some physicists shaken. But most readers were probably more interested in the closer-to-home matter of moving fast enough to make it into the house without getting mugged.

They would not be surprised at all to find that we're living in a crazy, permissive universe that doesn't pay attention to the laws we've set for it. And you never can find a policeman when you want one.

"The Law" always brings to mind policemen. But Law-and-Order as a political issue requires some detective work.

When did you first notice the Law-and-Order issue, ma'am? What did you understand it to say? Did you observe any particular identifying marks or, uh, color? You say it claimed it was going to protect you. And that was just before you felt this blow on the head and everything began going around and around. Yes, ma'am. Do you recognize the picture of this man? You say he's the one? Yes, ma'am. That's what it said under the picture of him we had in 1968. Thank you. You've been very helpful.

Identifications of Law-and-Order have varied from code-word-for-anti-black to deeply-felt-need-for-human-security. We need to find out what has been traveling under that alias, and what it has been doing.

The Law-and-Order issue has a double identity. It's the violence that raises the crime rate, and it's the "permissiveness" that raises the blood pressure. That includes pot, "sex," disrespect for authority, and general uppitiness of kids and blacks who used to know their places.

Official corruption and nice, high-finance crime don't get into the Law-and-Order lineup.

Senator Goldwater campaigned against "crime in the streets" in 1964. But much as people feared crime, they were possibly more afraid that Senator Goldwater might try to eliminate it with nuclear bombs.

Mr. Nixon campaigned for Law-and-Order in 1968 and left no doubt about the causes of crime. It was the fault of the Johnson Administration— and of the Supreme Court of the United States, which he labeled one of "the contributing factors" to a low percentage of crimes that "result in arrest, prosecution, conviction, and punishment."

Mr. Nixon also asserted that "we cannot explain away crime in this

196

HIGHER EDUCATION

1/10/69

HERE COME THE CLOWNS.

2/25/70

"FORWARD IN THE WAR AGAINST CRIME!"

11/30/69

"I SAY THAT WHEN THE STUDENTS START ROLLING IN 40 MM. CANNONS WE SHOULD FROWN ON THAT, EVEN IF IT MAKES SOME OF US UNPOPULAR."

5/1/69

country by charging it off to poverty. . . . The role of poverty as a cause of the crime upsurge has been grossly exaggerated—and the incumbent Administration bears major responsibility for perpetuation of the myth. . . ."

Said Mr. Nixon, "In short, crime creates crime, because crime rewards the criminal." The phrase "crime creates crime" was a little reminiscent of the gun lobby's famous saying, "Guns don't kill people—people kill people."

As an early step in reversing the policies of President Johnson and his Attorney General, Ramsey Clark, the new Administration, in July 1969, announced its opposition to federal gun registration and licensing of gun owners. Our society was threatened by "permissiveness," but not by the free-and-easy means of obtaining weapons of death, which every year injure 200,000 Americans and send 20,000 others to join a "silent majority."

Only a few months later this Administration showed that it was alert to the dangers that *really* threatened us.

In November 1969, federal officials seized ten drawings from a world-touring collection of erotic art by masters from Rembrandt to Picasso. The Department of Justice (under the new Attorney General that Mr. Nixon had promised to give us) labeled the seized works "obscene" and sought to keep the rest of the exhibition from entering the country.

The vigilant men now in charge of our government were determined that nobody in the U.S. was going to be raped by a Rembrandt or mugged by a Matisse.

True, the rate of violent crime in the United States kept going up. But Americans could be murdered knowing they were being done in with handguns in the good old American way. They were free from the fear of being bound and dragged off to a museum where they would be forced to look at erotic Picasso drawings which might bring on heart seizures.

The vigilance of the Administration in this area was underscored the following year, when it condemned the 874-page report of the Commission on Obscenity and Pornography.

This commission—authorized by Congress in 1967—found no necessity for legal controls on "pornographic" matter for adults, and no connection between so-called pornography and harmful behavior of any kind.

In a statement of hard-core politics, Mr. Nixon promptly labeled the two-year work of the commission "morally bankrupt."

An earlier report to President Nixon was made by the National Commission on the Causes and Prevention of Violence, headed by Dr. Milton Eisenhower. This one recommended urban improvement programs and other measures to get at the roots of crime. It also urged the confiscation of all handguns, except where there was a clear need for them, and registration of other guns.

This report was not condemned. It was ignored.

As for handguns, there are within the U.S. from 30 million to 60 million

"OH — AT FIRST I THOUGHT THAT
WAS MARIJUANA SMOKE!"

4/2/72

"TRAGIC . . . REPREHENSIBLE . . ."

5/28/71

LIVE AMMUNITION

5/6/70

END OF SCHOOL

5/19/70

of them in private hands—often with itchy fingers. Most murders are committed with them—including the killings of policemen and many of the assassinations of political leaders. Sales of handguns continue so brisk that the total is estimated to increase by two and a half million annually.

A year after the report of his commission, Dr. Eisenhower was still pointing out that the U.S. has "the highest gun-to-population ratio of any nation on earth," and is "the clear leader in violent crime," averaging fifty times as many gun murders annually as England, Japan and Germany together. In his non-political speech, Dr. Eisenhower also noted that progress toward financing an adequate system of criminal justice was "minuscule," and that "a lot of talk about law and order has been just talk."

One member of the Eisenhower commission (and a veteran of other such panels) said, "The problems of poverty, racism, and crime have been emphasized and re-emphasized, studied and restudied, probed and reprobed . . . I see nothing which is being done on the domestic front to eradicate the causes of violence." He added that "just as many children are going to be bitten by rats next year as last—and probably more."

But the Administration has been zealous in dealing with "permissiveness" and dissent.

On May 1, 1970, the day after his announcement of the invasion of Cambodia, President Nixon said, "You know you see these bums, you know, blowing up the campuses. Listen, the boys on the college campuses today are the luckiest people in the world—going to the greatest universities—and here they are, burning up the books, storming around about this issue. I mean—you name it. Get rid of the war and there'll be another one."

Three days later, students at Kent State University, Ohio, took part in an angry protest against the invasion. National Guardsmen who were called in after an ROTC building had been burned were taunted by students. Some of the students threw rocks at them. The Guardsmen fired into the crowd. Four students were killed and nine others were injured. Two of the four killed and some of the injured were not even participants in the demonstration. When the Guardsmen fired, none of the students was closer than 75 feet.

The comment of the President of the United States on these killings was the chilly observation that "when dissent turns to violence it begets tragedy." In response to calls for action, his Attorney General took a year and three months to declare that there was no basis for a federal grand jury investigation of the National Guardsmen. An Ohio state grand jury acted promptly to clear the Guardsmen and indict 25 students!

Less than two weeks after the Kent State shootings, another angry protest took place at predominantly black Jackson State College in Mississippi. Police fired a fusillade at students which left two dead and twelve wounded. Windows of a girls' dormitory were riddled with police bullets.

The Commission on Campus Unrest appointed by President Nixon re-

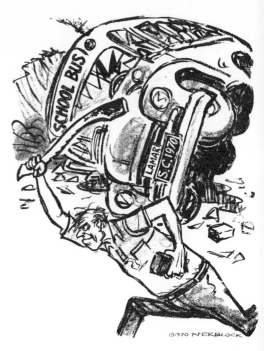

SON OF "SOUTHERN STRATEGY"
3/4/70

"GREAT SPEECH YOU MADE, CHIEF, ATTACKING THE COURTS FOR BEING TOO SLOW."
7/29/71

NO COMMENT
5/28/70

"IF WE BEAT UP A FEW MORE, MAYBE *WE'LL* GET INVITED TO THE WHITE HOUSE."
6/10/70

ported that at Jackson State, without previous warning of gunfire, twenty highway patrolmen and several city policemen fired nearly 400 bullets from shotguns, rifles, carbines and a submachine gun.

This commission's report in September 1970 found the Kent State and Jackson State shootings to be "completely unjustified." It blamed "racial animosity" of Mississippi police for the Jackson State killings. It said of Kent State that "the indiscriminate firing of rifles into a crowd of students and the deaths that followed were unnecessary, unwarranted and inexcusable."

But the President, who was engaged in the 1970 political campaign in which he was using the "college bums" and other young dissidents as an issue, could not get around to noting the commission's findings until after the November elections.

Incidentally, the "burnings" and "blowing up of campuses" were few, and in most cases seemed to be mysteriously unresolved happenings—especially considering the number of federal agents at work on campuses. Some young men stated publicly that the FBI urged them to act as provocateurs. At Ohio State University two "students" who played a leading part in touching off a clash between demonstrators and State Highway Patrolmen turned out to be undercover agents of the Highway Patrol itself.

Shortly after the Kent State and Jackson State killings, a group of New York peace marchers engaged in a non-violent demonstration in Wall Street. Nearby, hardhat construction workers indicated their intention to beat up these "peaceniks" if they dared express their views again in public. When a second peaceful march was held, the hardhats, in a not-exactly-spontaneous demonstration of their own, attacked the peace marchers. Shortly afterward New York hardhats staged a pro-war demonstration, and President Nixon invited their leaders to the White House. They had a happy visit and presented the smiling President with a hardhat of his very own.

When peace demonstrators have been guilty of any legal infractions, members of the Administration have compared them to Nazi brownshirts. Most such demonstrators were about as violent as Coxey's Army. And the less law-abiding demonstrators, however stupid or misguided, were certainly not engaged in persecuting anyone. But the leaders who saw many dissenters as "storm troopers," found nothing wrong with assaults on peaceful protesters by street gangs *supporting* Administration policies.

The lesson was not lost on Law-and-Order gangs elsewhere. Other groups of hardhats staged parades in which they also beat up a few people along the way—one of them the *mother* of a peace protester. She was watering her lawn as the war marchers were parading by.

These incidents evoked no words of censure from the White House, or from other members of the Law-and-Order Administration.

Nor were there White House words of censure a little earlier in the spring of 1970 when segregationists in Lamar, South Carolina, overturned two school

LAST RITES

8/15/71

LAW AND ORDERS

12/5/71

PERMANENT HOSTAGES

11/28/71

PATTERN

12/16/69

buses with children in them. If the President had made it clear that he upheld the law of the land on court-ordered desegregation, he might have offended groups who wished to overturn school buses.

In games of Cops-and-Robbers the cops are the Good Guys—or at least that's how it was when I was a kid.

Police have long been underpaid, and frequently undertrained and overworked. Their work is often dangerous, and many have given their lives in the line of duty.

My hat is off to all those men who perform so much service with such little reward. They, and all of us, would be better served if their forces were adequate and if they all received the recognition and compensation to which they are entitled.

But guardians of the law must also observe the law.

The Law-and-Order officials have played a game of Authorities-and-Dissidents, in which dissenters are the Bad Guys, and just about anyone with a uniform or badge of Authority is a Good Guy *regardless of his conduct.*

The evidence of this is not hard to track down.

The shootings at Kent State and Jackson State, which so significantly failed to stir the White House, were by men in uniform.

There have been other cases.

Police conducted pre-dawn raids on Black Panther headquarters in various cities. In one such raid in Chicago, in December 1969, Panther leaders Fred Hampton and Mark Clark were killed and four other occupants of the house were wounded. A federal grand jury found that only one shot could possibly have been fired from the Panther headquarters, while police may have fired as many as 99 shots into the house. No policeman was injured.

At Attica, New York, in September 1971, when prisoners protested against conditions they found unbearable, they seized 38 guards and other prison employees. Go-betweens, who talked with the prisoners, asked Governor Rockefeller to come to Attica. So did his State Corrections Commissioner. But he refused. After four days, he approved the storming of the prison block by about 1,000 officers, who went in with guns blazing. Forty-three persons were killed in this indiscriminate assault, including eleven guards within the prison. No hostages had been killed by the prisoners.

The White House promptly phoned congratulations to Governor Rockefeller.

Another rebellion occurred at Rahway State Prison in New Jersey less than two months after Attica. Governor William T. Cahill went to Rahway. He refused to use violence—or to promise there would be no disciplinary action. The rebellion ended within twenty-four hours with no deaths or injuries.

There were no reports of White House congratulations on Governor Cahill's action.

MINE VIGIL

1/9/70

THE UPPER DEPTHS

5/4/72

"IF YOU CAN'T LICK 'EM, JOIN 'EM."
7/22/70

OPENING GRANDSTAND PLAY OF THE SEASON

4/6/71

The trail of Law-and-Order even led into the United States Army, where the Commander-in-Chief intervened to have convicted Mylai murderer Lieutenant William Calley released from the stockade and returned to his quarters.

The reasons for President Nixon's clemency to Lieutenant Calley were probably political. But Calley was a man in uniform. It would be hard to imagine the President showing such leniency to a war protester.

Mr. Nixon also showed clemency in another case. He granted a pardon to corrupt union official Jimmy Hoffa—a man with political clout, whose union later endorsed President Nixon for re-election.

But Joseph Yablonski, who fought the corrupt union leadership of the United Mine Workers, had pleaded in vain for Labor Department supervision of the miners' election. His lawyer, Joseph L. Rauh, Jr., asked for protection for Yablonski after Yablonski had been slugged and nearly killed in full view of ten people following an election rally. Rauh was informed that protection for Yablonski and his family was not in conformity with FBI practice.

Shortly after the UMW election, Yablonski and his wife and daughter were murdered in their beds. The Labor Department finally decided to look into the UMW election. The Department of Justice then decided to look into the murder.

This takes us from the scene of the crime back to Washington.

The kind of thing that *did* seem to conform to FBI practice was given in a report from J. Edgar Hoover to the Attorney General in July 1970. Mr. Hoover characterized black extremist groups as the greatest threat to the nation's internal security, and warned that foreign influences were making inroads into the Panthers and other black groups.

He also warned that college groups were organizing and seeking time off from school *"to encourage the support of political candidates opposed to Administration policies. . . ."*

That's what the head of the FBI was reporting to the head of the Department of Justice while the rate of violent crime kept going up.

The Internal Revenue Service, in January 1972, acknowledged that it had set up a unit to collect information on extremist political organizations to find situations where there might have been tax evasion. The IRS didn't say how it defined extremist groups.

That's one of the things *it* was doing while crime marched on.

In this investigation of Law-and-Order we're now getting an idea of where the principals have been during the crime-in-the-streets. As for the Good Guys and the Bad Guys, you might not always be able to tell from their methods exactly which is which.

The Department of Justice claimed the right to tap and bug private citizens as it saw fit in "national security" cases, without court orders. It advocated no-knock entry into houses. It sought "preventive detention" to

"HE USED TO SAY IT WASN'T SAFE TO BE OUT ALONE HERE—NOW IT'S NOT EVEN SAFE TO BE NEAR A CROWD."

6/3/71

"BUT IF WE WERE ACTUALLY TO ATTACK THE CRIME PROBLEM, THAT MIGHT COST MONEY!"

1/2/70

"THE NEW AMERICAN REVOLUTION"

7/6/71

"RELAX, FOLKS—WE'RE WEARING WHITE HATS."

2/6/70

speed up justice by having people locked up simply on judges' guesses that they might be dangerous.

In the 1971 Mayday demonstrations in Washington, it engaged in massive arrests and detentions, in which it jailed 7,000 people, most of them without formal charges. And 36 hours after the initial arrests it was fighting in court to *keep* 1,000 of these people locked up—in most cases, still without formal charges. Of the 7,000 arrested, only about a dozen were tried and convicted.

The Justice Department at first said that the Washington, D.C., Police Chief handled the whole thing. But later, when private citizens filed suits, it became known that the "Mayday strategy" had been worked out with some of the highest officials of the Department of Justice.

This seemed to be the gang that couldn't shoot straight with the people.

What you have to keep remembering is that the Law-and-Order leaders are the *official* lawbreakers.

The Bad Guys are the protesters and dissenters, and the fussbudgets who don't like being picked up and thrown in the jug for going to work while demonstrators are in town.

Mr. Nixon has even tried to expand the powers of the Subversive Activities Control Board, so that it can decide for us which are the *organizations* we should avoid if we don't want to be considered Bad Guys.

Preventive arrests, preventive detentions, wiretapping—all these things are cheaper than promoting justice by spending enough money on courts, on police, on speeding up the judicial process, on cleaning up crime-producing conditions and on reforming the prison systems which breed more crime.

On this score, Judge Tim Murphy of D.C. Superior Court in Washington said, "We spend more in this country on peanut butter than we do on criminal justice."

As far as that goes, the government probably even spends more to keep food from being grown than it does to keep crime from growing.

Let us jot down on our detective notepads: ITEM—Requested spending for the entire federal court system for fiscal 1973: $189 million; for the federal prison system: $181 million; ITEM—Cost of the price support programs for agricultural commodities for 1973: $4.3 *billions*—most of this for not growing certain crops.

That's not peanut butter.

Talk about Law-and-Order is cheap—much cheaper than crime prevention. And political attacks on the courts are cheaper than support for them.

In government prosecutions, it's also easier and cheaper to charge conspiracies than to prove overt acts. Any two or more people can be conspirators, especially if they're dissidents. They don't even have to be Black Panthers or members of other "New Left" groups. The federal government has been throwing in more and more conspiracy charges lately. Among the more prominent

"RIGHT, CHIEF—IF WE GO AFTER
EVERYBODY, WE'RE BOUND TO HIT
A CRIMINAL SOME TIME."

3/15/70

"THIS LATEST GOOD-NEWS REPORT
COMES TO YOU DIRECT FROM OUR
OFFICIAL UNDERGROUND
BUNKER . . ."

9/12/71

"WE'RE AGAINST CRIME, BUT WE
DON'T WANT TO INTERFERE WITH
PRIVATE ENTERPRISE."

2/16/71

cases have been those of Anthony Russo and Daniel Ellsberg of the Pentagon Papers, the principals in the "Berrigan case," and those in the "Dr. Spock case."

As for the latter trial—Roger Baldwin said that lawyers for the American Civil Liberties Union had to introduce the alleged conspirators to each other in the courtroom. Conspiracy convictions against some of the "Spock defendants" were overruled; charges against the rest were dropped.

In the Berrigan case, the Department of Justice came up with a special combination-offer conspiracy charge. It accused the defendants of conspiring to kidnap Dr. Henry Kissinger, to blow up heating system tunnels in Washington, and to raid federal offices. In this combination deal, even selling the jury on the raiding-draft-board charge was apparently supposed to put across the whole conspiracy package.

It didn't.

The jury found the Reverend Philip Berrigan and Sister Elizabeth McAlister guilty of passing letters out of prison—a minor charge. But at least nine of the twelve jurors found the conspiracy charge too much to swallow, and a mistrial was declared. The government's star witness was a paid FBI informant who was a convicted confidence man and self-confessed liar. The defense alleged that he acted as an *agent provocateur*.

One Justice Department lawyer said in court that the Reverend Philip Berrigan and his friends are a bigger threat to the nation than organized crime.

That's what a Department of Justice lawyer said in court while organized crime flourished—and while more Americans than ever were being robbed and raped and mugged and murdered in unorganized crime.

Some sharp Law-and-Order detective work might reveal that there *are* a couple of conspiracies in this country. One is composed of the people who believe in the Bill of Rights and who exercise the rights of free assembly and free speech.

The other is made up of people who band together in dingy surroundings —a conspiracy of those who do not get out into the country, or even to country clubs, to live clean, healthy lives.

It is the conspiracy of the poor.

Goodness only knows why these people prefer to be poor and live in slums and ghettos—or, for that matter, why they prefer not to hire the best lawyers when they get into trouble, like the well-to-do. They ought to get themselves better courts and more policemen too, because the crime rate is higher in their communities than in the affluent ones. They don't provide themselves with good schools and other improvements either. This can't all be coincidence. It must be a conspiracy.

They are also engaged in an economic conspiracy. Statistics show that more of them are unemployed than upper-class Americans—although recently some engineers and other nice people have tended to get themselves

"YOU'VE DONE SUCH A GOOD JOB, WE'RE TAKING YOU OFF THIS BEAT."

12/14/69

"WE JUST WANT TO TAKE YOUR CLOTHES SO THAT WE CAN WEAVE YOU A WONDERFUL NEW OUTFIT."

7/8/69

"WE ARE FOR SPEEDY COMPLIANCE, BEARING IN MIND THAT THERE'S BEEN ONLY FIFTEEN YEARS TO DESEGREGATE THESE SCHOOLS."

7/6/69

TAP

5/16/71

involved in unemployment too. The conspiracy of the poor may be spreading.

Some of these same people who congregate in slums and ghettos and at employment offices and welfare offices also tend to congregate in prisons and penitentiaries. It is a mark of their conspiratorial nature that many of them spend much of their lives in dark places.

The success of this conspiracy is shown by the fact that while crime has always been heavy in the slums, it is now extending to the suburbs and rural areas. That shows what clever conspirators can do. The government could cope with them by spending money to improve the inner city areas. But as Mr. Nixon proclaimed in 1968, the connection between poverty and the upsurge in crime has been something of a myth.

The conspiracy of the poor is plain, and the crime statistics prove it. But many of these conspirators somehow think they have the same legal rights as anyone else.

Let's see where we are now in our detective work.

The Law-and-Order fellows are the ones who believe in tapping and bugging without warrants; who break into houses without knocking; oppose effective gun controls; lock up and detain people without charges; and keep track of people's ideas and associations to see that they don't think wrong thoughts. The forces of Law-and-Order also bear down on those conspirators who insist on staying poor and living in hovels.

All clear so far? Well, here's more:

Besides wanting to avail themselves of rights in criminal cases, some of the non-affluent think that laws to protect them in other ways are also valid.

For example, in 1965 Congress passed a voting rights act to insure that those who were being deprived of their right to vote in certain states should be free to exercise the franchise. But they are just the kind of people who might use their voices to do what J. Edgar Hoover cited in his memo to Attorney General Mitchell: "support candidates opposed to Administration policies." Since 1969, this voting law has not been enforced as vigorously as it might be.

Law-and-Order people sometimes find *court* orders inconvenient. For example, court orders on desegregation have been interpreted by White House loose-constructionists as excuses for raising the political specter of "massive busing" to enforce a "racial balance," which the Supreme Court never called for.

Also troublesome to Law-and-Order officials has been the U.S. Civil Rights Commission, headed by the Reverend Theodore Hesburgh, president of the University of Notre Dame. It issued a unanimous report in 1971 that cited as "grossly inadequate" the civil rights performance of the federal Law Enforcement Assistance Administration, which administers grants to local law enforcement agencies.

It said, "The President's posture . . . has not been such as to provide the

"IT'S FOR SECURITY—IT MAKES US
FEEL MORE SECURE."

3/14/71

"THIS TAP HAPPENS TO RUN A
LITTLE SLOWER."

11/19/70

"THERE'S ONE THAT MIGHT WANT
TO MAKE A CAMPAIGN
CONTRIBUTION."

4/16/70

"YOU LOOK ALL RIGHT TO ME—I
SEE NO REASON TO PROSECUTE."

5/29/70

clear affirmative policy direction necessary to assure that the full weight of the federal government will be behind the fight to secure equal rights for all minorities."

Of course, people who hold views like that often say that court rulings are "the law of the land" and that ours is a government of laws, not of men. But Law-and-Order authorities know that voters don't elect laws, they elect men. Such authorities naturally feel it is up to them to decide—in an Orderly manner—which laws to enforce against whom, and which laws to violate. True Law-and-Order men do not shrink from this responsibility.

It is the same way with official information and "leaks." Somebody has to decide what to look into and what to give out.

The White House announced in 1970 that one of its political appointees had been authorized to have the Treasury Department send him any income tax returns he requested for his examination.

Again we have the authorities faced with decisions, decisions, decisions.

Whose tax returns to give special attention to? What stories to put out about whom? Should government officials look into the cases of Democratic officeholders or of Republicans? These are hard choices.

Senator Joseph Tydings of Maryland (Dem.) was the subject of a *Life* magazine article in August 1970, which charged that he had used his official position to increase his personal fortune by influencing the outcome of a $7 million government loan to a private company.

It was not until two days *after* the November election that the Administration "cleared" Senator Tydings of those accusations.

Unfortunately, Senator Tydings had just been defeated in his bid for reelection.

But charges and investigations and clearances all have to be done properly and thoroughly—and at just the right time. There is an Order in these things too.

Sources of money have been of great concern to the Law-and-Order people. Since money in the wrong hands is the root of much evil, they have tried to make sure it gets into the right hands.

In the 1968 Presidential election, Mr. Nixon and his campaign manager, John Mitchell, reached a new national peak in political campaign funds. Such funds are supposed to be reported before the election to the clerk of the House of Representatives as required by the Corrupt Practices Act. The Nixon funds were not so reported.

Attorney General Ramsey Clark passed the matter to J. Edgar Hoover for investigation. After a long and Orderly investigation, Mr. Hoover passed it along to John Mitchell, who by then was in charge of the Department of Justice.

Attorney General John Mitchell carefully studied the case of Nixon Campaign Manager John Mitchell and found no reason to prosecute anyone

MILK RUN

9/29/71

**"THERE DOESN'T SEEM TO BE
ANYTHING FROZEN HERE."**

10/15/71

**"FOR PRESIDENT? WE SEEM TO BE
SUPPORTING NIXON—BUT WE
DON'T WANT TO."**

10/1/71

for these violations of the Corrupt Practices Act. In a Law-and-Order Administration that's the kind of difficult decision that has to be made by men at the top.

Another such decision was made by President Nixon, who in 1970 vetoed a bill passed by Congress to control campaign spending for broadcasting.

Law-and-Order officials appreciate the contributions citizens want to make toward maintaining a Law-and-Order Administration. A nice Orderly arrangement of political contributions involving President Nixon and lobbyists for farm dairy groups was detailed on September 27, 1971, in stories by George Lardner of *The Washington Post* and by Jerry Landauer of *The Wall Street Journal*.

Mr. Lardner's article recounted how various lobbyists contributed money for the re-election of Mr. Nixon through dummy organizations—often unknown to people who lived at the addresses listed as headquarters for these "organizations."

"There must be some mistake!" exclaimed an investment broker whose home was listed as the "Organization of Community Volunteers." This was one of 68 committees, some of which bore titles like "Americans United for Political Awareness" and "Supporters of the American Dream Committee." Twenty-five committees were listed in Washington, D.C.'s Union Trust building, which showed not a single one on its directory. "This sounds like something that doesn't smell right" said a woman whose home address was listed as headquarters for another "organization."

Perhaps the prize name among these dummy organizations was "Committee for Political Integrity."

More interesting than the exotic listings of committees was the sequence of events leading to the dairy-farm lobby's many-splendored and many-titled contributions to the Nixon fund. As related in Mr. Lardner's September article:

> The three dairy farm lobbies in any event began their 1971 GOP contributions last March 22. . . . The donations came just 10 days after Secretary of Agriculture Clifford Hardin announced there would be no increase in milk price supports for 1971.
>
> Leading dairy farm spokesmen met with Mr. Nixon at the White House March 23. On the next day, March 24, Hardin announced a price increase of 27 cents per hundredweight, saying that "continuing research had turned up new information on rising farm costs."
>
> Other contributions came in the following weeks. . . .

I did three cartoons on this political "milk run" that ran up hundreds of thousands of Nixon campaign dollars by milking the taxpayers and consumers of millions. But nobody else seemed to be greatly stirred by the articles at the time. Four months later I was relieved to find that I was not a hopelessly Old-Fashioned Boy. In January 1972, Ralph Nader filed suit for

"CALL MRS. BEARD'S DOCTOR—
THERE'S BEEN A TERRIBLE ACCIDENT."
3/22/72

"FIRST THE GOOD NEWS, MR.
PRESIDENT—YOU WANTED THAT
$400,000 CONTRIBUTION STORY OFF
THE FRONT PAGES . . ."
3/23/72

"THINK OF YOURSELF AS
CONTRIBUTING TO 'THE NEW
PROSPERITY.'"
11/25/71

a rollback of the milk support prices, charging that they were raised by the Nixon Administration as a payoff for campaign contributions.

Mr. Nader also charged, in another lawsuit, that Attorney General Mitchell and top administrative officials of the Senate and House had "caused and encouraged wholesale, widespread and flagrant violation" of the Corrupt Practices Act, and "fostered corruption, fraud and dishonesty in the electoral process."

As the reader can see, the Law-and-Order issue *does* require some detective work. Much of it has been done by investigative reporters who want "just the facts, ma'am."

Newsday, the Long Island newspaper, published in October 1971 a series of articles on land and business deals involving former Senator George Smathers, Charles G. (Bebe) Rebozo, and mutual friend Richard M. Nixon. Among other things, it found that at a time when President Nixon was selling 185,891 shares in a Rebozo-dominated land firm for $2.00 a share, "other stockholders still were buying the shares at $1.00 each." It quoted one of the other owners as saying of Mr. Nixon's sale at 100 percent profit, "He was President and we thought we ought to give him a fair price."

Fair is fair—and turnabout is fair play. *The Miami Herald* reported on October 25, 1971, that Mr. Rebozo was given four chances to bid on, and win, a $233,315 government contract—despite lower bids.

But these newspaper stories aroused less general interest than later magazine and newspaper articles involving the operations of the Department of Justice, the White House, and particularly Mr. Richard Kleindienst, who was the subject of Senate hearings on his nomination to be Attorney General.

Life magazine reported that in 1970, Harry Steward, the U.S. Attorney in San Diego, squelched an investigation of several San Diegans, including a close friend of President Nixon, for conspiring to violate federal tax laws and the Corrupt Practices Act. The U.S. Attorney had been appointed on recommendation of Mr. Nixon's friend, the Nixon fund-raiser.

The same U.S. Attorney quashed a grand jury subpoena against another prominent Nixon fund-raiser, and later admitted that he had done this because the fund-raiser was going to recommend him for a judgeship.

All this was glossed over and covered up by Deputy Attorney General Richard Kleindienst—who later conceded that U.S. Attorney Steward had shown "poor judgment"—and by Assistant Attorney General Henry E. Peterson, who later acknowledged that Mr. Steward was guilty of "highly improper conduct." But top Law-and-Order officials Kleindienst and Peterson had merely admonished Mr. Steward privately.

In another interesting 1970 incident, it turned out that Mr. Kleindienst had been offered a bribe by a political acquaintance, Robert T. Carson, to block a criminal prosecution. Mr. Kleindienst testified in court that Carson had said "he had a friend . . . who was in trouble," and if Kleindienst could

WHITE HOUSE EMERGENCY SQUAD
3/29/72

4/21/72

4/30/72

**"I DO SOLEMNLY REFRESH MY
MEMORY AND TRY TO RECALL TO
THE BEST OF MY ABILITY . . ."**
6/2/72

help, the troubled friend "would be willing to make a substantial contribution of between $50,000 and $100,000 to the re-election of President Nixon."

Mr. Kleindienst and Mr. Carson continued with their conversation. But a week later, when Mr. Kleindienst learned that the FBI was investigating Carson and planning to put him under electronic surveillance, Mr. Kleindienst suddenly realized that he had been offered a bribe by Carson and reported it to the FBI.

Mr. Kleindienst was a very busy man and one who sometimes forgot things. So did other Administration officials, big business executives and lobbyists who testified during the hearings on Mr. Kleindienst's nomination.

One of the things that made the hearings particularly interesting was the disclosure by columnist Jack Anderson of a memo reportedly written by a lobbyist for International Telephone and Telegraph.

It indicated that high government officials were involved in the settlement of three anti-trust suits against ITT at the same time that ITT was generously offering to contribute $400,000 (or $200,000 or $600,000) toward the 1972 Republican National Convention.

This was a coincidence that many people found fascinating. Another was the fact that following the disclosure of the memo, ITT—overcome by a sudden urge for spring housecleaning—ran great batches of papers in its Washington office through a shredding machine. Some weeks after publication of the memo, and after the spring document shredding, officials of ITT (and the ITT lobbyist) decided to declare that the memo was not authentic.

Acting Attorney General Kleindienst, who had previously said that the ITT settlement was "handled and negotiated exclusively" by former anti-trust chief Richard McLaren, refreshed his memory when questioned by a Senate committee. He found that he had indeed met with ITT executives at various times and had arranged for them to meet with him and the chief of the anti-trust division. When they stopped to think about it, other officials recalled meetings and arrangements, too.

When Acting Attorney General Kleindienst returned to the hearings for one last day of testimony, he seemed able to remember little about anything: "I don't recall . . . it made no impression on my memory . . . I've got the haziest recollection . . . it just doesn't stand out in my memory . . ."

One of the most interesting memory lapses was that of former Attorney General John Mitchell, campaign manager for Richard Nixon in 1968 and for President Nixon in 1972—until he bowed out in mid-year. Regarding the original selection of San Diego as the site for the 1972 convention, Mr. Mitchell in his testimony referred to "the Republican National Committee or whoever decides those things." The billion-dollar Hartford Fire Insurance Company, which ITT was allowed to keep under its settlement with the government, was "Hartford or whatever the name of the company is."

Even with the memory-refresher courses provided by Senate committee

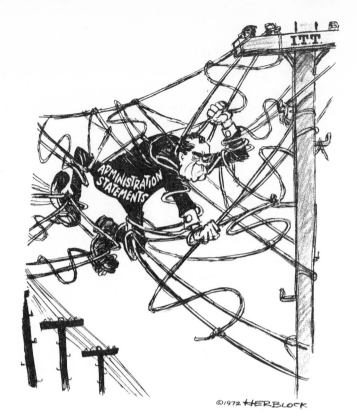

TANGLED WEB

4/7/72

TILT

6/6/72

members, there were still so many discrepancies between statements of Administration officials that they could not be resolved before the hearings were banged to a close by Senate Judiciary Committee Chairman Senator James O. Eastland—an ardent supporter of former Attorney General Mitchell and of Mr. Kleindienst.

For example, White House aide Peter R. Flanigan, who had solicited an outside report on the ITT case from a New York investment banker, testified that he and Mr. Kleindienst had conversations which Mr. Kleindienst previously asserted had not taken place.

As to the reason for soliciting the outside report which helped to change the mind of anti-trust prosecutor McLaren, Mr. Flanigan said, "I was merely assisting another overworked public servant."

With public officials so overworked that they need assistance from a New York investment banker to help them decide billion-dollar anti-trust cases, it's no wonder they can't remember everything.

What ordinary people don't realize is that important officials who are busy providing Law-and-Order for the nation can't be expected to keep in order their recollection of niggling little details about a few hundred thousand here, a billion there.

Senators and newspaper writers don't always realize either that Law-and-Order officials can take care of all the investigating of Americans that is necessary, without anyone else's help. But people get caught up in the spirit of detective stories and get curious about facts and details.

In mystery movies, all the strange goings-on are unraveled in the last scene, with a rapid-fire explanation of everything that's happened and who did exactly what. It would be nice to be able to do the same with the ITT case and all the other strange cases involving the Administration and big money. But accounts of government officials and their activities don't always lend themselves to that kind of ending, as do stories of violent crime.

Ah yes—the violent crime we heard so much about a few years ago! When last reported, it was climbing higher than ever.

Big contributions to the campaigns of high government officials have also been climbing higher than ever.

And however mysterious the political-financial arrangements of government officials may seem, we can take comfort in the fact that these things have happened under an Administration completely committed to Law-and-Order.

Thank goodness for that! If they'd happened under some other Administration, we'd have had cases of Corruption in Very High Places. ∎

"OFFICER, I WANT YOU TO
INVESTIGATE — UH, NEVER MIND."
4/27/72

"WHO WOULD THINK OF DOING
SUCH A THING?"
6/20/72

"REMEMBER, WE DON'T TALK TILL
WE GET A LAWYER."

6/21/72

"TELL THE HOUSEWIVES WE ARE
CONTINUING OUR FIGHT AGAINST
INFLATION."

3/31/72

"THERE'S THE TIGHTEST SECURITY
OF THE CAMPAIGN."

6/18/72

"STRANGE – THEY ALL SEEM TO
HAVE SOME CONNECTION WITH
THIS PLACE."

6/23/72

"COME BACK AFTER THE ELECTION
– I'M KIND OF TIED UP RIGHT NOW.

7/19/72